BEYON
SYRIAN ARMY

A ROAD MAP TO SUCCESS THROUGH AMERICAN TECHNOLOGY

SYRIA

VAHAN V. BASMAJIAN

M.I.T. GRADUATE
MASSACHUSETTS INSTITUTE OF TECHNOLOGY

About the Author
Vahan V. Basmajian

Vahan was born in Aleppo, Syria, from parents who escaped the Turkish massacre of the Armenians. He was brought up in a multi-cultural environment and began learning several languages in elementary school. His parents' history, along with the suffrage trying to build a new life in Syria, influenced him the most. He learned about Middle East history and attended Christian schools while having Muslim friends in high school. His exposure to the turbulent life in Syria, political upheavals, and war-time environment forced him to think about freedom.

After graduating from Aleppo College, he was drafted to the Syrian Army, where he planned and succeeded to escape into the US Embassy in Beirut. Once free, he entered the United States alone with plans to build his future through American technical education.

Mr. Basmajian followed a career path that earned him the "Invention of the Year" award from the Society of Professional Engineers in the US. He is committed to tell his life story to high school students and to teach them how to develop a sense of direction and follow his footsteps to become a productive citizen of the US.

In the year 2000, Mr. Basmajian served in an advisory capacity with the Massachusetts Renewable Advisory Trust (MRET) by invitation of then Gov. Paul Cellucci. Additionally, he served on the advisory board of public schools and university engineering departments for graduate students. He has conducted seminars on the subject of alternative fuels for many years. He holds a Master's Degree in Aeronautics and Astronautics with a major in Rocket Propulsion from Massachusetts Institute of Technology (MIT).

Mr. Basmajian traveled to many countries with the Governors of Massachusetts on Trade Missions and is a strong believer in education and training for all people. He is dedicated to bringing out the best in each student and motivating each one to future career paths.

In Appreciation

1. My true friends in Aleppo: who saw the path of blood and tyrants—and helped me escape

2. "No name-no thanks" letters ever to be written back to one person who asked me not to name him: silence, pride, and hope that drove us into success

3. My parents: who were the first to *escape* the Turkish massacre of Armenians and set a good example for me to endure and build a future

4. *No-name* gentleman in the US Embassy in Beirut: who allowed me to enter the United States—despite his knowledge of my *passport* "issues"

5. Dr. Richardson of Massachusetts General Hospital: who gave me my first full-time job to support myself and loaned me money to pay my tuition at Wentworth Institute in Boston

6. Dr. Eugene Covert: who opened the doors for full-time job at MIT and mentored me throughout my graduate work-study program and the starting of Megatech Corporation

7. My community friends in the United States: who *did not* discriminate—regardless of my background, religion, or race—but encouraged me to carry on toward the career path that led me to success

8. Governors of Massachusetts: Special thanks to Gov. King (D), Gov. Weld (R), and Gov. Cellucci (R) who personally helped Megatech and I through trade missions and exports to many countries

Dedicated To:

The next generation of young students and the concerned parents
who care about their children's career paths,
individual freedom, and respect for life

Part I
Life in Aleppo:
Escaping the Syrian Army

Part II
Succeeding in the United States:
Discovering American Technology

Part III
Your Move:
Technical Career Paths in Alternate Energy and Automotive Industries

Overview

This book has three parts to it, because it represents the true story of the author. The story begins with his birthplace in Aleppo. He tells his life as it happened during this period: from childhood, to graduating from high school, and his escape from the Syrian Army. The author describes what it took to survive and succeed in the United States and how he got involved with America's Energy Independence goals. He concludes the book with valuable data and information which students/readers can use for years to come.

Part I: Life in Aleppo: Escaping the Syrian Army

My birthplace is Aleppo. It is where I grew up, graduated from high school, and was drafted into the Syrian Army for training. I am telling the *true* story as it occurred in my life: from first grade to the last day that I was in the Syrian Army. I tell in great detail how we planned and executed the *escape* from the *army* to *Lebanon*.

The risks were very high for what I did when there were no other options given by the Syrian Army:

(1) get trained and be sent to the Israeli Border as part of an "ambush group"—literally a suicide mission, or

(2) escape the country: if caught—a certain execution!

Both choices meant death if failure occurred.

The intent of this section is to show how goals can be accomplished based on someone's upbringing, family history, values, and experiences in growing up among various people with different cultures. These factors that made me a strong person and allowed me to have faith in myself, build confidence, and make decisions. Now I live in the United States and hope to inspire the new generation of high school students—either born here or overseas—to take action and be decisive about their future.

Part II: Succeeding in the United States: Discovering American Technology

I entered the United States with only $125; yet, I achieved my goals through education and training. In this section, I describe a series of jobs I had through college and how I developed a career path. I wrote about my background to show young men and women the "no-excuse approach" in achieving goals through education and training. I built my future on America's technical education. It is one of the foundations for becoming a productive person and contributing toward job creation.

Part III: Your Move: Technical Career Paths in Alternate Energy and Automotive Industries

The road map I offer in this book is a career path that leads the person into the energy, power and automotive industries. I hope that both parents and guidance counselors participate with the youngster's future career development—using this book as a guide. The bottom line is that it is *best* to make the person productive rather than have him or her depend on the government. A nation's strength is the sum of all individuals who are productive citizens: no matter if you live in the United States or overseas. I provide sufficient facts regarding alternate energies, renewable energy sources, and non-carbon-based energy supplies. This should help both the American public and the student make intelligent decisions about America's energy independence. Part III could be used as a resource book for any high school student who wants to continue toward higher education or specialize in a technical field for which there is a high demand

Technology Then: Aleppo Citadel over 4000 years ago

Technology Now: MIT

Table of Contents:

Part III:

YOUR MOVE: | 75

Technical Career Paths in Alternate Energy and Automotive Industries

Part I
Life in Aleppo:
Escaping the Syrian Army

1. Growing up in Aleppo

As an immigrant, I dedicate this true story of my life to all young students who are born in the US or who are immigrants who need to get a sense of direction. I would like to make one important point: I *was born in Syria* from *Armenian parents who emigrated* from Turkey. *But…*I call myself "made in the U. S. A."

Yes, I am a "product" of the American technical schools that set the foundation for my career:

- As a technician, an Associate's degree from Wentworth Institute in Electrical Engineering

- As an engineer, a BS degree from Boston University in Aeronautical Engineering

- As a graduate engineer, MS degree from Massachusetts Institute of Technology (MIT) in Aeronautics and Astronautics

How lucky? *No*. Just follow how it happened as far back as my memory serves me: to my first grade in a Catholic school. Remember, I was born into the Armenian Christian

In Aleppo Syria, Vahan attended and received his sixth-grade diploma from Per-Balian Jesuit Elementary School

Orthodox religion, yet I was surrounded by over a 90 percent Muslim, Arabic-speaking population.

What about my parents and grandparents? They were from the "*old*" country. In my eyes, I saw Turkish-speaking parents who had escaped the Turkish massacre of Armenians that were fighting for their independence. Now I see their struggle and how they are surrounded with various cultures. However, this causes a conflict in my mind, and it makes me think:

My grandparents lived in the "old" country without electricity or freedom and escaped for their lives. But what *jobs* could they find in an unknown country and not starve?

My parents had to learn more languages—Arabic and French in addition to their Armenian language—to survive. France was ruling Lebanon and Syria at the time when the First World War started. What choices did my father have in terms of *jobs*?

No doubt, my mind was not capable of handling all of the stories being told to us children—four boys and our two sisters—about why we were forced out of the "Old Armenia:" now under Turkish rule. What about the 1.5 million Armenians that were massacred? My father told me, "I saw the cut throat of my brothers, and my sister was burned in a church." "But why is it," I asked my parents, "that Christians and Muslims could live centuries together, yet when it comes to freedom, they have to be killed?" So I told my father, "I am going to be trained when I grow up to learn the use of arms and fight for our freedom." My father's answer was simply, "Get your education—the only way your generation will survive."

2. Gunpowder: a Mix of Technology and Culture

What can a ten-year-old do when it comes to *guns* and *technology*? My father became a real resource for information, because he had a book binding/printing company (an amazing story of an entrepreneurship to be discussed later). Whenever he printed or bound books of interest, he read them. So I engaged him with questions:

1. "Dad, how can the wheels turn on a car from just liquid gasoline?" He tried his best to explain, and I tried to relate. This began my interest in automotive technology.

2. "Dad, what's in these wires that gave me a jolt?" I asked after playing with electrical outlets and getting my first shock from a wire I tried to plug in. This, of course, prompted a discussion about electricity. Another incident that impressed me was when he took me to one of the power-generating plants in Aleppo that was operating with huge diesel-engine generators.

3. "Dad, how could a "charcoal" have so much power?" It was gun powder: another example from which I learned when my uncle used it in his long barrel hunting rifle and I saw it fire. Wow! Certainly it brought to me science and chemistry as he explained how gunpowder is made.

Well, it was time to learn and experiment. By age eleven, I managed to make my own gunpowder. By age thirteen, I fired my first hunting rifle and a 9mm handgun made by Browning of Belgium.

Let's return to the topic of school: that is, middle school, which I attended after graduating from the only private Jesuit school in Aleppo. However, the middle school and high school were run by Protestant missionaries who were teaching the Bible and English language. Now there was more conflict in my head: I was born into the Christian Orthodox Church, attended a Jesuit elementary school, and ended up with Protestant teachers while surrounded by Arab Muslims in my class! It did not take me long to realize that these Muslim students were the children of a famous rich Muslim family: all half-brothers. They would rather come to a private missionary school than go to public Muslim schools. Once again, I added one more conflict into my life. The Arab Nationalism, under the leadership of Gamal Abdul Nasser of Egypt, made Syria become a part of The United Arab Republic with Egypt. In my high school, we came under new guidelines: Arabic language study of the Koran for one year became mandatory. I learned a lot about their religion and social structure and families, and I learned *not* to approach Muslim girls for a "date" or even ask for social time. By the age of seventeen, I was in total conflict: a cultural *war* had begun within me. Religion, the politics of Arab Nationalism, and *freedom* were all combined in one classroom.

A student council was formed to encourage student interaction. Instead, it became a focus of violence. Student groups were formed to protect their own cultures and interests. Now we call them "gangs" of youngsters. Within days, one of my Muslim classmates pulled a knife on me. In my quick reaction—self-defense—I knocked him onto the ground, took the knife out of his hands, and gave him a black eye with a solid punch to his face. I knew retaliation was coming soon: by the next day or two. I managed to alert my friends and get ready for a confrontation. I put my Browning 9mm gun on my belt and another revolver on my side. I was determined to defend myself, my friends, and my values to the end. They got the message and rolled back.

Graduating from Aleppo College in 1956, with a high school diploma, before being drafted to the Syrian Army

Left to Right: Vasken, Vahan, Hovhannes, Vahe (Photo taken in Aleppo, Syria)

All four brothers were born in Aleppo, Syria, from parents that escaped the Turkish massacre of Armenians in Marash, Turkey. My parents set an example of family, education, and cultural values and seeded the spirit of freedom! All four brothers grew up with a strong desire to build their futures and be successful. All of us, except the oldest one (seated with eyeglasses), found our way to get to the US and be very successful. My oldest brother's family is somewhere in Aleppo.

3. Syrian Army: Call for Training

High school graduation was marred by the total destruction of the Egyptian Army during the Suez War of 1956. Within days, all high school graduates were called into duty to serve the Syrian Army and get immediate training to fight the "Imperialistic armies of the West and the Israelis." I had no choice but to report and go for training at the eastern edge of Aleppo that leads into vast areas of land and desert.

Massive camps of young high school graduates in the thousands were camped under tents. Certainly, there were all kinds of characters: a mix of various beliefs, tribal kids, Christians, Muslims of different sorts, etc. There were chants and

Vahan seen with his French made rifle in the Syrian Army

prayers for Allah and officers who were there to help them become martyrs in fighting the Israeli "Satans."

I was in my tent, trying hard to sleep, when I started thinking about what my father and mother had gone through when they had escaped the Turkish massacre of Armenians. My brain started boiling with thoughts of this clash of values while my fellow Muslim "martyrs" were praying loudly!

9

The Camp tested my willpower, my ability to re-evaluate what my parents had gone through, and what I had to do to free myself. I had  to *escape* the camp and get out of the country—but how? It was surrounded by military guards ready to shoot or beat you to hell. Now I was grinding away about where my life was heading. The biggest issue kept coming back—based on my values and future plans toward good education, training, and careers. I started filtering in my mind what to do about my camp and military service; we were being trained and told to kill the "Jews" and "throw them into the Mediterranean Sea." Yes, I lived with fellow soldiers who prayed to *God* for the opportunity to revenge the Israeli attacks and the killing of *Islamics*! While my fellow soldiers were praying in their tents, I was evaluating the options and choosing the values of what my parents believed in and what they did to escape the massacre. Yes, they kept telling us that what we needed were:

"Jobs, education, and freedom."

I started thinking that the Israeli-Arab conflict would end up in the massacres of two races and nations: similar to what the Turks did to the Armenians. My conclusion? Plan an escape to freedom! It took me from the ages of ten to nineteen to evolve into a person with conviction, values, and courage to achieve the great escape plan of my life to the US—where I would shape my own destiny.

Fellow trainers with various cultural and religious backgrounds marching in harmony

4. Life at the Military Training Grounds

Several thousand young men were at this base, which was outside of Aleppo: about twenty miles east. The sounds of joy for Muslim fanatics, prayers, and the shouting of victory slogans slowly faded away when the Sergeant called the group members (about twenty-five to thirty men) to start marching in the desert for training. A military march? Lucky for me, I was trained as a boy scout from the age of twelve. I could not believe my eyes that the Sergeant was showing us how to keep the arms straight out at shoulder level, while the opposite leg went with firm knees. Does it sound simple? It wasn't simple for several guys who got confused with the instructions of matching left hand movement to the right foot forward. At times, these guys were "thinking" how to match the left with the right. Instead, they were moving the left arm with the left foot. This really looked both funny and bad. After a few swear words by the Sergeant, some guys still did not get it right. So, the Sergeant decided to use force: he took his rifle and poked it into the body of one and used the "butt" end of the rifle to clobber another one. I could not believe my eyes when one trainee got hit on the head and was bleeding. I couldn't control my emotions at seeing this young Muslim student being mistreated and called "*himar*" (donkey) on top of it all! My natural reaction was, "He is not." I barely got the words out, when he dashed on me with his rifle and asked me to crawl like a *kelb* (dog) on the ground. I was bleeding from my elbows; the Sergeant wanted to use me as an example *not to pity* fellow soldiers during training. There was no more doubt in my mind that he wanted total control over us, to break our spirits, and to cause us to become soldiers who were willing to kill.

The following few days it appeared to me that the purpose of this *rushed* training was to get us ASAP to the Israeli border. The Syrian Army with Russian weapons was told to move their forces—including new trainees—to defend the homeland, Syria, from the Israeli attack that was imminent. After all, in the weeks before Egypt's Army was destroyed in the 1956 Suez War, surely the Syrians believed they were next.

My group was ordered for weapons training. We ended up in a rifle range with live ammunition. About one hundred meters away, we were told to use the bolt-action rifles (thirty odd six-barrel sizes), to aim, and to fire. Yes, ten in a row, we lined up and fired! The noise was so loud that some of my fellow trainees had completely missed the target board that was at least two yards-by-two yards in size with bull's-eye markings. One guy had wet pants: the noise and fear were too much for him to control his bladder.

I did not think very smartly. The Sergeant came to me and said, "You hit three out of five into the bull's eye. Where did you learn how to use rifles?" I felt like an idiot that he might be able to press on and discover that I was a member of a revolutionary party against Russian control of the government. Fortunately, his pride took over, and he wanted to show his group that he was better than they were. He stood up and fired the gun in a standing position—instead of lying down on the ground. Well, he did worse than I did. So, then he said to me, "I will recommend to my supervisors that you be sent to the Israeli border as a sharp shooter in a team of five soldiers."

My mind was crushed with the thought that I would kill a few Israeli soldiers and then be killed! It sounded like a suicide mission. Now I had no more doubts and no more time left to plan the escape.

5. How We Escaped the Camp

The top officers ordered the breakup of "cliques" within the tent residents so that no friendships could emerge and become a social group. In the worst case, maybe a conspiracy could have developed in which politically friendly soldiers might have worked against the government. This was either a case of paranoia or military discipline that took me by surprise and caused serious concerns. I had to be moved into another tent and join new characters.

Another setback was the horrible condition of water and food. I had no choice but to eat what was given to me. A soldier brought in a five-gallon pail filled with food that was foreign to me. My plans to escape took a setback when I came down with food poisoning. I was taken to the camp's military station for observation. I missed a couple of days due to my illness. My body had gone through two major shocks: my elbows were taped (due to the bleeding as a result of their harsh treatment a few days before the food poisoning), and now my body was not up to full strength.

My initial friends in the first tent were moved for the same reason I was moved: to break up the social ties—or whatever they thought to be the case. My brother, who was a year ahead of me in high school, had to report for military service. Yes, we were able to reconnect. With one other Arab Christian, we started the escape plan. The perimeter was well guarded, and we looked for places that could be "weak" at best. We were very aware that these guards were brutal and had orders to shoot.

The fear was deeply rooted in everyone's minds. After few meetings, we found the weakest point in an area where the bathrooms were located. I must admit, when you got a backhoe, dug up trenches, and put wooden planks to walk over it, it was filthy! The trench and its smell were horrible: some guys had gone outside this area in the open space to have their bowel movements. The military guards were *avoiding* this area—I do not blame them—due to the horrible conditions: both on the grounds and in the air. Now that we had found hundreds of trainees going there at early morning hours and many roaming around the bathrooms looking for a convenient location, we decided to melt into this crowd and take advantage of it. So the first step of the *escape plan* was ready: walk and look like one of them going to the bathroom.

The next step involved our uniforms. A soldier could not be seen outside of the barbed fence in military uniform. We had to look like civilians and find our way back to Aleppo. We saw a farm about a mile away, with a few farmers in the fields. The idea came out clearly: let's look like the farmers' helpers—a regular *Arabian* farmer look. But there was one huge problem: we all had *pants* rather than the Arabian robe. So, I talked nicely to my "tent-friends," and I asked if I could borrow or buy some of their spare Arabian clothes? They were more than happy to give us their clothing; however, the farmers had their "head-dress," which no one had in the camp. We had no choice but to come up with the idea of using towels to put over our heads and wrap them around to look like a "turban" headdress. This was the best we could do—given the circumstances. The time had come to execute the plan.

In the early morning, we carried our Arabian robes and towels and pretended to go for our morning constitution—where many people were buzzing around. We drifted slowly: as if looking for a "clean area" to do our business. Yes, we took off our military uniforms, put on our new dresses, and crawled under the fence. The guards were not anywhere close to see us in the morning dusk. Wearing our head-dresses and kneeling down as if we were farmers worked as planned. I said, "Guys, keep down and walk farther toward the farm—as if we are the helpers."

Sure enough, we got to a distance that was out of the guard's clear vision. Certainly, he did not want to kill farmers. At this point, our walk became faster toward the country road that the camp had built for easier transportation. We found the road, a few cars went by, and we let them go; our plan was to find a bus or truck to go by, and we would wave them for a ride. This was a common practice for villagers who wanted to get into Aleppo. We were concerned that the bus might not show up fast enough, and the morning head count would show us missing from training at the camp. Fortunately, a truck carrying fruits to Aleppo stopped. The three of us jumped into the back of the truck and got to Aleppo.

We knew we must act as soon as possible with an escape plan: *run out of the country*—but how? It was *wartime*, and the government announced that military rules would replace civilian rules. As a result, all the buses and trains were stopped, and the Syrian Border was closed for all civilian travel. *No* more buses were running: only limousines for special people with special permits. I found out the facts with great disappointment when I personally went to the bus station where most travelers to Lebanon went to purchase a ticket. Now, I knew how tough it would be to cross the border into Lebanon, because Egypt was in a state of war against the French, British, and Israeli armies in 1956.

Russian T-64 Tank—Russian weapons were very common:
both in Syrian & Egyptian armies

6. Planning the Escape to Lebanon

Immediately, I contacted my friends, who were members of the same political party, older, and tuned toward security forces. They gave me excellent insight as to what to do next.

In Aleppo, my parents and my oldest brother had print shops and bookbinding businesses. This turned out to be one of the best things in my life when I found out that my oldest brother was invited to the "secret police" headquarters to bind files that were truly of high security. This police force was known as the *Deausieme Bureau*—the "Second Bureau." They had power over the police force, dressed in street clothing, and spied over civilians. Our party members were very scared of them; suspicious behavior was enough cause to be arrested. Yet my oldest brother, being Armenian Christian, was selected over "other" Muslim businessmen. His service to bind the *secret* documents got him into very close ties with the Chief of the *secret* police—let's calls him Chief Ahmad. He gave a lot of respect to my brother. I wondered how I could benefit from this relationship—not right now, but later when I was in the *escape* limousine.

My political party friends started assisting me by offering contact names for certain purposes. To cross the Syrian border during wartime—with my military age and full name recorded in the military camp—was a monumental task to overcome. We all agreed that physically running across the mountains to Lebanon could be of very high risk. Certain people had succeeded, but getting caught or being fired at was another matter. The smugglers' route was discovered by the border troops (called *Gendarme* from the French language: they were known to come from different countries and were brutal in their nature). This option was out, but the next best plan was to *create* documents that looked real: as if they were from the military. However, once I crossed into Lebanon, I had better end up in Europe or the United States. This required a *passport*, which Syria stopped issuing in order to control the outflow of business-men or certain people that were held as political hostages.

There was not much time to debate, but I had to make choices: if I were caught, I would be imprisoned or *shot* as a traitor. What about my friends that were part of the team to get me out? Under torture, they forced you to speak up and confess. I knew it was *now* or *never* that I would get this chance, because it would be only days before the military staff would look for me. (After fleeing into Lebanon, they did that by knocking on the door of my home and asking for me.)

7. Conspiring to get the Passport

How would I cross the border with a passport to the United States? That was a sure sign of escape to a non-friendly country, and it guaranteed arrest. Per my connections, I went to see the "*insiders*" at the proper offices that were *not* issuing any *passports* to the public. My contact name showed up, and I stated who I was; I made it clear that I had come for a special purpose. He looked at me and said, "Let *God* be with you (in Arabic)," after giving me an envelope that had what I needed: the *passport*. To *this day*, I keep it as a bible (or key) to my freedom. When I opened the envelope, it was written for both the United States and Europe. This meant if I went to Europe and then to the United States, it would be fine. The passport was prepared by my political friends and looked authentic. It did not matter to me, but if I were ever discovered by the police or Border Guards, it would be certain disaster.

I had to act very fast, because if we were discovered, the group that was helping me would be rounded by the security forces. Now I had the *passport*—without a visa to enter the US—but I could show it at the Syrian border. The first question would be, "How did you get this passport?" And I would reply, "I am at a military age of eighteen and must be in the Army."

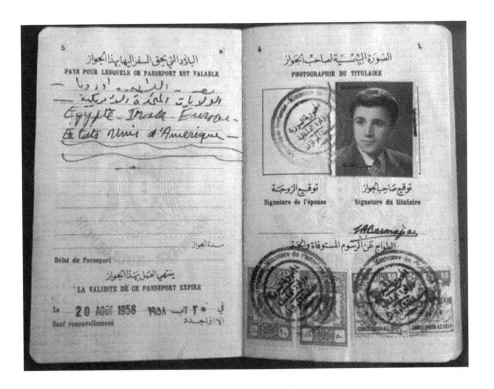

8. The Break-In into the Commander's Office

The second challenge was what to present at the Syrian border to the *Gendarme* (the no-nonsense, tough border patrol officers). Again, the insiders and my political brothers came to help. One such person was a Christian Arab who had just graduated from law school and was arrested for being "pro-Western" and a possible danger against the state. The government sentenced him to forced labor in the Army Headquarters to be a secretary to the commander—based on his pro-Western views, law degree, literacy, and skills. They took him out of any political activity. The government miscalculated the spirit of the people who are educated and ready to take exceptional measures for their rights. He was stripped of his rights and turned into a servant in the hands of the officers and the Commander of the base.

What he conceived was a perfect plan to get me out of the border crossing: "I will give you a permit from the Army to take courses at the American University of Beirut and to be trained to become a medical technician for the battlefield services." Since there was a shortage of medical staff at the Israeli border, it made a lot of sense. But *who* would get the papers ready and make it look real? Any forged papers that could be analyzed could put you in front of a firing squad. He calmly answered, "Come with me in the early morning hours, and I will give you genuine papers." I asked, with apprehension, "What about the seal of the Commander?"

We set the date to meet at the entrance of the building and planned a "break-in" into the Commander's desk. He was known to the guards as a "secretary" to the Commander, so it was no big deal: both of us entered at early hours to get a head start. He went right to my file and showed me that I was tagged as "*Spy* to the British." He told me it was just a matter of days or weeks before they would take someone out of circulation: just as it had happened to him. I was literally shaking, while he was tearing the documents and destroying my file. Then he took the "Special Permit" paper, opened the Commander's desk, took out his seal, and stamped it!

God, I could not believe what I saw: real documents in my hands. He told me to never call him, thank him in a letter, or try to communicate. If caught, we would be dead. "Run for your life. When you cross into Lebanon, give this note to my girlfriend, and *do not* acknowledge me directly or indirectly. That is the favor I ask you to do." I did it with success.

Time was running out. At this point I had: (1) a "forged" passport (as the Syrian government would say), and (2) a "forged" military permit (as the Syrian Army would say).I knew I had better pack right away and hope that this plan would work. I rushed home to pack and only let my family know. I took enough items to only look like I was going to a University as a medic trainee from the Army.

9. Final Good-Bye to my Parents and Aleppo

We were now at the limousine station with my father and mother asking them to keep calm. None of my brothers or friends were there. "Dad, let's make this look normal." **"Fine, my son."** After all, he had traveled on foot over thirty days escaping Turkey to Aleppo from the Turkish massacre. He had an "iron" heart and willpower.

About seven of us got ready to board the stretch limousine. It looked like very special people were getting on board. There was a very wealthy Saudi, a couple of businessmen, and a young man (about twenty-eight to thirty years old) with Western clothing. I was in the middle, and this gentleman sat next to me by the window. So, I was "trapped" on each side: by this young man and another businessman. Windows were open, and as soon as the engine started, both my father and mother had tears pouring out of their eyes. This was not part of our plan! I took in my emotions and tried to control them. The limousine pressed on to start the journey, and I was the youngest person among the seven passengers. Was I ready to take the challenge at the border? I had the military permit ready as a legal traveler. Tucked inside my underwear was the passport to the United States.

After about a half-hour drive, we left Aleppo, and that within a six hours' drive, we should be at the military checkpoint/offices where all documents, baggage, etc., would be checked and approved to go on, or I would be arrested as an illegal escapee from the Syrian regime.

The young man, let's call him "Samir," introduced himself, and I did the same. He asked me what was taking me to Beirut/Lebanon.

I told him, "I have been chosen (as an honor) to become a Medic at American University of Beirut (A. U. B.). How about you?"

"I work for the Secret Police, "*Deausieme Bureau,*" in Aleppo," he replied calmly.

"Good for you," I murmured, and then I asked him, "Do you know the Chief?"

"Of course I do. Do you mean Ahmad?"

I told him we were very friendly with him, because my brother had a contract to enter the Secret Room so he could bind the files. This man, I call him Samir for convenience, was telling the truth: how else would he know him so well? My brain was in turmoil and thinking the worst: he was riding the limousine to arrest me while I showed my papers at the border crossing—that was it!

Could I run away when the limousine stopped halfway to gas-up or to rest? I thought that maybe during this time I could pretend to use the bathroom, and through a back door, I could disappear somewhere into the town. True nightmare scenarios were pouring in and out of my head: "What if the driver does not stop at all? What are my options? Maybe when the car stops in traffic, I could make a sudden hit to his head, open the door, and run for my life(the last words my friend murmured when we successfully broke into the commander's office)." My fears were increasing, because the driver did not stop, and escaping from the car was no longer an option.

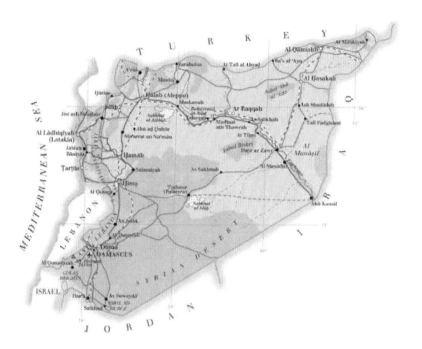

10. Syrian–Lebanon Border: The Moment of Truth

The six-hour journey to the exit checkpoint was within sight. I kept reminding myself to stay cool and look like a military trainee who was a "chosen" person and deserved to be serving the Syrian Army.

The Border Guard, the so-called *Gendarme*, came to the limousine and asked for papers (permits); I gave my paper permit. The secret police next to me, Samir, gave his <u>card,</u> showing that he worked for the internal security of Aleppo. Samir and the *Gendarme* walked together to the office to verify all the passengers' papers. My heart literally stopped—if they were to call the military headquarters to ask for verification and they said, "No," I was done! I was certain Samir was there to arrest me in the act—with solid evidence that I was an enemy of the State. The evidence was in their hands. I just knew I would be sent back to Aleppo for *execution*! I kept thinking that Samir had a card: just like a driver's license. He was real and would come back with handcuffs. One minute…five minutes…. Time went by, and the worst wait of my life was draining me. I did not know what they were doing inside. The other passengers were not my concern—especially Saudi business people that must have had legal passes to Lebanon.

I noticed the checkpoint building doors opening, and Samir—joined by the *Gendarme*—had my papers. He asked me to open my luggage. I wondered if they were looking for my passport to the United States—which was hidden in my underwear. If they ever found this passport, it

would certainly be more than enough evidence against me to prove that
I had:

(1) committed treason against the Syrian government, and

(2) broken into the Headquarters of the Syrian Army, stolen the
Seal of the Commander, and falsified permits.

The above offenses call for the death sentence!

The *Gendarme* searched my luggage thoroughly and found no weapons: nothing but clothing for my stay in a dorm at the University. He
looked at my eyes and said, "Allah Mayak ("let God be with you.")."

The limousine started the engine and entered the neutral zone
between Syria and Lebanon. I started a conversation with Samir (the
Syrian Secret police officer). The Lebanese Border Guards were in sight.
Then, Lebanon was pro-Western, and I knew that I was safe and that
Samir *could not* arrest me while I was in a neutral zone; nor could he arrest
me in Lebanon. If anything, I could use self-defense against him with
no retaliation from the Lebanese authorities. I was like a time bomb:
ready to explode! I wanted to know who Samir was, and I thought to
myself, "I will ask him when I am past the Lebanese checkpoint."

The limousine stopped at the Lebanese checkpoint; all of us had to
show our papers again. There were no problems. We were greeted with,
"*Ahlan oua Sahlen* (Welcome with peace)."

Samir and I were standing outside of the limousine, and the Lebanese
Guard was watching us for something going on between myself and
Samir. I finally decided to tell Samir (the secret police bastard) the truth
about my mission.

"Samir, I am free. I am not going to Lebanon but to the United
States. Finally, I am out of the Syrian Army's jaws—ready to shape
my own destiny," I told Samir, who I thought was ready to arrest me
throughout the ride into Lebanon.

Samir's answer was, "Hey, I am escaping to Venezuela—even though I am a secret police officer assigned to Lebanon."

Apparently, he had been sent to organize/hunt down anti-Syrian elements in Lebanon, and that was why he had shown his badge at the Syrian crossing. I hugged him as a *hero*!

He told me, "I knew there was something about you. I knew that your assignment by the Army to study and become a medic was a cover-up."

I asked him how and why he became suspicious of me.

He replied, "Your father and mother were crying when the limousine was leaving Aleppo. They should have been overjoyed, rather than crying…."

I thought he was a damn good Secret Policeman, and he deserved to be out of Syria—just like I did!

11. My Entry to the US Embassy in Beirut

I did not waste any time, and overnight, I went to the US Embassy for a visa to the United States. Within an hour, a consulate senior-staff member came to see and interview me. Within a minute, he said to me, "You should be in the Syrian Army; what are you doing here, and how did you get here?"

I explained and revealed the fact that I had fled the Syrian Army training camp and barely succeeded in crossing the border alive. I expressed my desire to go to the United States where I could be safe and build my future. He got right to the point:

"What party did you belong to?"

"What high school did you go to?"

"Give me your family's names and addresses and contacts where we can check your background."

I was revealing well-kept secrets and showed him my true goals and desires. I told him that if I ever got caught and sent back to the Syrian Army, I was *dead*.

The Embassy officer commented about my English: "It is not too bad. I will need about two to three weeks to check you out. Come back to see me then."

The interview was well on track. I waited, until he asked me only one question that shook me up:

"How did you get this passport? We know the Syrian Government does not issue passports—especially now at wartime."

I was totally honest and upfront: "My political friends helped me get my passport."

He told me that all of the information I gave him came out to be true during my background check in the past three weeks.

"Your passport is not legal; however, given the circumstances, I will accept it and offer you a 'student visa' to the US."

I thought, "My God—now I can move on into my journey plans and start a new life."

Part II:
Succeeding in the United States
Discovering American Technology

12. The Journey to Freedom: New York City

I left Beirut, Lebanon, on a ship and picked up an ocean liner in Greece to cross the Atlantic. The voyage was an emotional yo-yo. I was not facing yet what was ahead of me in America. I had no idea what was out there in New York City and the rest of America.

I was alone….

Aleppo and Syria were no longer visible.

I was looking ahead as we cruised the ocean.

My thoughts of the past were holding me back! I felt like being a runner in one-hundred-meter dash at the Olympics, yet I was looking backward to see what was behind. "It does not matter anymore," I kept reminding myself. The images of my parents, relatives, and the political friends who took risks on my behalf—and hundreds of others whom I had known since my childhood—came and went just like waves in the Atlantic that was passing by the ship. I had no choice; I was on my way to the United States. I must plan to succeed, as I had planned my escape from the Syrian Army. My motivation started increasing when I thought of the potential rewards waiting in America. I wondered: "But where that will be? How do I get there?"

Many days went by with endless thoughts and dreams, until the ship arrived in New York City. The US customs agents had thousands of pieces of luggage to look through, people to be checked, and passports to be verified. I was still apprehensive about my passport that was from

Syria. What if someone were to raise questions as to the validity: knowing that Syria *did not* issue passports to the US?

My heartbeat increased. I had no choice but to stand happy on a land where I could build my future. Then, yes, I was approved by the customs agent, who stamped my Syrian passport: showing a student visa. Now I was alone, standing among thousands of pieces of luggage and people. I picked up my belongings and looked around the vastness of the city.

"Where do I go? No one is here to say 'hello' or to greet me."

I was lonely!

"Which direction is it to the YMCA?"

Yes, I needed a place to stay and get ready for America. I had only one hundred twenty-five dollars in my pocket—that was three months' income for a teacher in Syria—yet, it would not get me too far in the US.

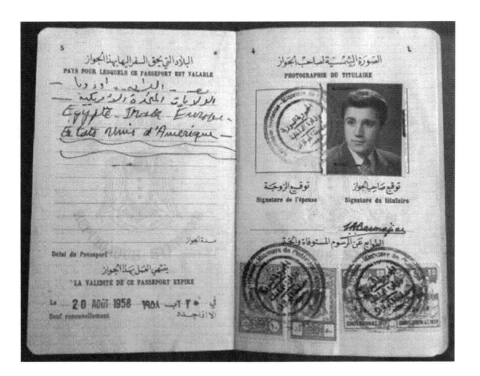

13. Facing Reality: Planning for a New Life

Standing in New York City and observing my surroundings, I saw: tall buildings, busy roads, traffic lights, people rushing everywhere, subways, and taxis going by. I needed to get moving; I was in America. I waved a taxi and asked him, with my heavy accent, "Please take me to YMCA." Fortunately, it was not too far away, and I stayed for three days. The taxi fare alone cost me the equivalent of three days' pay in Syria. At this rate, I was worried how fast the money would be dissipated—then what would I do? The three days at the YMCA gave me the time to digest the new facts of life.

I signed into the YMCA in New York City and started my initial plans. I knew the first thing I should do would be to walk around and get a feel for the people and the environment. Certainly, I was not a tourist, but I was in search of facts about America. I saw thousands of cars, shoppers, and traffic lights that were not in use when I was growing up back in Aleppo.

I went back to the room to start thinking: what were the next steps I needed to take to move on from New York? I surely got my thoughts and confidence back without concerns about the Syrian secret police hunting down pro-Western "elements," as had happened in Syria. The feeling of *freedom* and the sense of security gave me the self-confidence to develop my first action plan:

(1) where would I go from New York City;

(2) where could I find a room to rent;

(3) could I find any kind of job that would generate enough income for survival;

(4) what college would accept me on a short notice/application; and

(5) where was the Armenian Community that could provide me some guidance?

I had no knowledge about roads or highways. I had no driver's license in America, and I had no one to show me or direct me out of New York City. After the second day, I decided that time was **not** to be wasted, because it was costing me dearly every day that went by without a decision. Decision?

After all, I had been able to make my own decisions in Aleppo that had dealt with life and possible *death* by hanging or execution. I thought it was time to choose, and I went to the registration desk and asked how far it was to Boston. The attended replied: "By bus, maybe five hours—depending on where they stop." I thought Boston sounded like my best bet. I thought, "Go for it!" After all, I knew from Aleppo that there was a large Armenian Community, organizations, and many colleges that could fit my needs. The Immigration Law was very clear: I had *only* a student VISA—not an Immigrant visa that would allow me to work legally and stay as long as I wished. A student visa required that I show my full-time studies at a college to be legal. So, the best choice for me was to go to Boston.

The bus station was not too far from the YMCA, and I took the ride and prayed for the best in Boston. I hoped I would meet some Armenians or relatives that I could find. I remembered my father talking about one of his sisters that survived the Turkish massacre (yet one was burned alive in Marash, Turkey). I knew her name was Elmast, and she lived in Watertown, Massachusetts, but I had no idea what she looked like or how I could find her.

The bus driver announced, prior to arrival, the name of every major city for passengers to get off. After four hours or so, I heard the word "ooster." I thought the bus driver meant, "Boosten:" a real mix-up of accents. I got off the bus in "ooster," which turned out to be "Wooster." (Its real spelling is "Worcester.") What did I know? In America, Worcester was called "ooster" by a heavy-accented bus driver! This was my second lesson: listen well and learn the English language as fast as I could. After rescheduling my bus trip to Boston, I arrived and found my aunt. What a success!

Staying at a relative's house saved me money. But I needed to make more money—immediately. I asked if there were any kind of work. They told me that yes, there was. It was in a small restaurant/grocery store owned by an Armenian. I became his helper to serve food and wash the dishes. Wow—I was earning about two to three dollars per hour, including tips. Every hour's income was the equivalent of a day's pay for my parents. Another lesson I learned: earn and spend wisely.

The time had come to set guidelines for myself, based on the American way of life—or something different. I was comparing it with my past in Aleppo and growing up with Muslims in a "closed" society. So, I had to come up with certain parameters and priorities. This was the only way of life I knew. So, I made list:

1. Economic conditions: how can I earn money?

2. Educational institutions: how much tuition is required?

3. Rooming and meals: should I buy or cook?

4. I need to consider my physical health and the emotional stability needed to face my age group of guys or girls, with their concepts and perceptions about me.

5. How will I achieve the social life needed to bring acceptance among the nearby neighbors and my new friends?

I remember well when I was asked if I had ever driven a car or a *camel* in Syria! If I could absorb the punishments in the Syrian Army training camps, questions such as this one were a small bump in my social life. My answer was, fortunately, "I have done both!"

Instead of writing a long book or history of how I found jobs, I will list the jobs I took to earn money. The funds were necessary to meet my daily needs to survive and build a new life in America.

14. Climbing up the Ladder

My success and survival heavily depended on finding jobs—regardless of how small or big. The following jobs led me from my college years to my professional positions.

Job #1: Dishwasher

I worked at a small restaurant and Cabot Farms in Somerville, Massachusetts. It had a three-hundred-seat capacity for weddings or special occasions on weekends; it was always busy with functions. It turned out to be a blessing for me. I had another job during the week at Massachusetts General Hospital (MGH). Also, I worked the night shift at American Bilt-Right Company. The clock-hours combined were about eighty hours during the summer season. The Cabot Farms job added another eight hours per weekend. This made my weekly hours total about eighty-eight to ninety-two hours. It hardly left any time to have social life. After two weekends at this wedding hall, I noticed that American weddings have a "standard" program: first, a reception; then, dinner, followed by a band and dancing. I decided, "Well, why look for girls anywhere else? They all come here well-dressed; enjoy a nice party and have fun! I've got it! Now I can bring my three-piece suit, tie, and dress shirt, and when the band starts playing and everyone starts dancing, I can change out of my kitchen clothing, put my suit on, and just mix in with them!" Wow—it worked! One wedding had a lot of Armenians in the party, and I met a family that was speaking Armenian. I introduced myself (after listening to their private gossip) and told them I was Armenian: "Sorry, ladies—I understand what you are privately talking about." They were shocked and then asked, "What are you doing here?"

My answer was that I worked weekends there, the second shift at Massachusetts General Hospital, and I went to Wentworth Institute during the daytime. They could not believe that I could work at Massachusetts General Hospital and be able to go to college full time. To test if I really worked at MGH, one lady (I found out later who she was) said to me, "I have a niece that is studying Nursing at MGH, and she is here; I would like to introduce her to you."

This was what I had been waiting for and had been hoping would happen. I wanted not only to work and earn money but to meet potential girlfriends. Yes, she was beautiful—nineteen or so—and I had a meltdown. It had been a long time coming to meet such a nice girl. She was well-dressed for the wedding, and checking me out, she asked me, "Where at MGH do you work?"

I replied, "At Vincent Research Lab, under Dr. Richardson. If you don't believe me, come and see me Monday at 6:00 p.m."

Yes, she showed up at 6:00 p.m. with some fruits in her hands to share with me in the Vincent Research Lab. My little plans and initiatives worked wonders. In earlier months, at the Armenian Church, I had met other girls. Now, this was the third one, and her name was Sandra. Her dorm was the next building over, and I did not have to travel to see her. I thought, "Am I seeing the true fruits of my hard work, or is America full of fruits—just like a supermarket?"

Wow! She became number one on my date list. She graduated from the nursing program at MGH, received a BS in Nursing from Boston University, and earned a Master's degree from Northeastern University in Boston. She is still my wife after <u>fifty</u> years of marriage. We now have three children and grandchildren.

My wife Sandra, graduating from Nursing School

I have given you a detailed account of my start-up jobs in America, my early social life, and my strong desire to get things done "right." Any mistakes would cost me a <u>lot</u>, and I could not afford it. After all:

(1) my parents were in Aleppo and could not help me;

(2) I was alone and working to pay my rent, utilities, and food;

(3) I had to pay my own college tuitions; and

(4) I needed to keep healthy—physically and emotionally—so that I could earn money.

Job #2: Massachusetts General Hospital (MGH)

I went to interview for a Lab Tech position I saw advertised. I thought it was a technical type of work—like an engineering tech.

I met Dr. Richardson, who showed me the lab. What a shock— it was an animal lab for cancer research! They had hundreds of mice, rabbits, etc. He told me that there were certain chemicals that needed to be injected into these mice, and there were records that needed  to be kept as to dosage and date. When I saw the needle being inserted in the back of the mouse (along the spine, about one inch from the tail toward the neck), I felt chills on my spine. I remembered my high school when typhoid disease was spreading. The nurses and doctors came to the high school to give *mandatory shots* to every student. My reaction and dislike for needles had made me <u>jump out</u> of the window and escape the school!

Dr. Richardson looked at me and said "Now it is your turn, and I expect you to fail the first time. The needle can hit the mouse's spinal cord and paralyze it." I felt paralyzed myself, but I *needed* a job to support myself. I told him I could do it…and did it!

"You are qualified and start your job next Monday. By the way, where are you from?" At this point, I was hired and there had been no discrimination at all. I told him the truth: "I escaped the Syrian Army, and I must support myself and be ready for tuition payment in September. This job will make me economically independent." Dr. Richardson asked me if I had sufficient funds for my first semester. I told him I had only half the amount.

Right there and then, he took out his checkbook and "loaned" me the money. I am sure he was showing deep sympathy. His social conversation got me to the point where I told him, "I am dating a nursing student from this hospital." He thought that was cool and suggested we could all meet in the near future. Sure enough, Sandra came after work and I introduced her to him. Dr. Richardson was a famous surgeon at MGH, and my girlfriend, Sandra, had just gotten her job to work in the operating rooms. I could not believe what a blessing it was that he got to know Sandra as she assisted him in cancer-type of operations, while at the same time, I was working with mice for cancer research. Dr. Richardson was single, and he volunteered to tell me that he intended to get married the following year. He asked me if I like Sandra enough to get married. My reply was, "Now she is number one among three girls I had met earlier." Yes, I beat Dr. Richardson to the altar.

Wedding Day for Vahan & Sandy, December 27, 1959

Delayed honeymoon celebration in Beirut, Lebanon, in the summer of 1960

Job #3: American Bilt-Right Corp, Chelsea, MA

Within months, I got an invitation to Dr. Richardson's wedding. We now have a common bond and mutual respect. Many years later, one of his kids grew to be sixteen and worked for me at Megatech Corporation. Looking back at the years, I can say that a "mousy-looking" job turned my life around! Now I say to young students: "Do *not* look down on a job! Take it; you will see the benefits down the road."

It is good-hearted Americans—such as Dr. Richardson, with his open-minded attitude—that gave me an opportunity to work and turn my life around.

Could I use more money at that point? Yes, so I decided to look for something that would fit my available hours. This company had a job opening in the third shift during the summer season. School was off, and I was holding the job at MGH during the day shift. But when college started, I moved the MGH job to second shift. This job added more money, because it was the night shift: ending at 7:00 a.m. I had just enough time to run home, shower, and go back to MGH until 4:00 p.m. This gave me five hours of sleep until 10:00 p.m., and I went back to my night shift. This extra income gave me such a positive feedback that I was energized, and I could go on to the next day and follow the same process. This was all thanks to America!

Job #4: Electric Motor Repair Technician

I managed to finish my studies at Wentworth Institute of Boston, and I got a job as a technician. My Associates Degree helped me earn more money. The pay rates were higher, and now I was exposed to *some* engineering principles and better income. The logical progression was to extend my education into a full-blown engineering degree. I thought, "Why not?" I married Sandra the same year we both got our degrees. Now we had two engines to run on and generate income. She encouraged me to go after my BS degree in Engineering. I did it, and that opened more doors for me. I kept saying, "What a country America is; there is no end to the opportunities!"

My visa changed from student to permanent when I got married, and five years later I became a full citizen of the United States. After the citizenship ceremonies, I told my wife I had gone beyond the Syrian Army and truly discovered America!

Job #5: Research Engineer at MIT, Cambridge, MA

Certainly with a BS degree in Aeronautical Engineering (Design Major) from Boston University and later a Master's degree in Aeronautics and Astronautics (Rocket Propulsion Major) from MIT, I felt like I was in a world of technology, and the supermarkets were in Boston. How and why I developed such an appetite for American Technology can be traced to ALEPPO.

I wrote earlier that when I was a ten-year-old in Aleppo, my father showed me how to make gun powder, and I learned about electricity and how cars run. For the first time, I started to think that the roots of my success came from Aleppo, and with deep conviction, I could state that being born in Aleppo turned out to be an asset.

I thank all my friends and teachers in Aleppo, where I drank their water and ate their bread. Thanks to my pro-Western friends that gave me courage to exit the political jaws and dictatorial powers of the government. I have never hated Syrians—just their policies and those who were stripping *human rights* from everyone!

JOB #6: Secret and Top Secret Missile Era

After completing my research work at MIT and having very good knowledge of hypersonic flights and missile aerodynamics, I had five offers from major aerospace companies. Was this luck or just a *reward* for my hard work and *positive* attitude toward opportunities?

I do hesitate, from this point forward, giving details about my jobs; however, I will continue giving my subsequent jobs and positions that are non-classified. My deepest gratitude goes to Dr. Eugene Covert, who was the Director of Aerophysics Labs at MIT, for opening the doors and giving me the opportunity to prove myself. Yes, he mentored me throughout my professional years—even as of this writing. He offered his time and shared his vision to get me into higher professional levels that I could not ever dream about from Syria.

Job #7: President and CEO of Megatech Corporation

My current biography for Megatech Corporation reads as follows: Mr. Basmajian is the CEO and co-founder of Megatech Corporation. Since 1970, he was the president and treasurer for Megatech, and during his service, he managed to take the company public. He held patents in Nuclear Reactor Training, Hydro-electric Power Generator Demonstrators, Wind Turbines, Steam Turbine Generation, an oil-less Alternative Fuel 4-Cycle engine, and a Geothermal Heat Pump. The latter patent won him and Dr. Charles Haldeman (co-inventor) the Invention of the Year award in the United States from the Society of Professional Engineers in 1985.

In the year 2000, Mr. Basmajian served in an advisory capacity with the Massachusetts Renewable Advisory Trust (MRET) by invitation of then Governor, Paul Cellucci. Additionally, he served on the advisory board of both public schools and university engineering departments for graduate students. He has conducted seminars on the subject of alternative fuels for over thirty years. He holds a Master's degree in Aeronautics and Astronautics with a major in Rocket Propulsion from Massachusetts Institute of Technology (MIT). He is currently re-designing the world's first oil-less engine which he invented in the early 1970s to operate with hydrogen, in addition to what it was designed for (ethanol, methanol, gasoline, propane, natural gas, or any liquid/gaseous fuel). His pioneering ideas have contributed to the advancement of alternative fuels with traditional 4-cycle engines. He is heavily involved in organizing workshops and training students toward America's energy independence.

As CEO of Megatech Corporation, he has been active in research and development since the founding of the company and has introduced many new products. The inventors for the patents listed below are Vahan V. Basmajian and Dr. Charles W. Haldeman, who offered the patents rights to Megatech Corp. The trademark MEGATECH© is registered in the United States and many foreign countries. GEOPUMP© was a trademark for the company's heating and cooling system and the name of one of its divisions.

The following patents were granted by the U.S. Patent office to Dr. Charles Haldeman and me. Both inventors are graduates of MIT, from the Department of Aeronautics and Astronautics.

Self-Lubricating Piston	US Pat. No. 3,890,950
Transparent Oil-Less Engine	US Pat. No. 3,698,370
Gas Analyzing	US Pat. No. 3,895,915
Nuclear Power Demonstrator	US Pat. No. 4,216,593
Wind Power Generator	US Pat. No. 4,087,927
Turbine Demonstrator	US Pat. No. 4,073,069
Electro-Mechanical Dynamometer	US Pat. No. 3,789,659 System (for various sizes)
Oil-Less Transparent Engine	Japanese Patent No. 984,578
GEOPUMP© Energy System	Canadian Patent No. 1,166,242
Wavy Tube Heat Pumping	US Pat. No. 4,556,101
Geothermal Heat Transfers	US Pat. No. 4,566,532

Mr. Basmajian copyrighted many of the alternative-fuel student manuals which are available only through Megatech Corporation, located at:

MEGATECH CORPORATION
525 WOBURN ST, Ste. 3
TEWKSBURY, MA, 01786

Telephone: (978) 937-9600
or visit the website at: www.megatechcorp.com

Remembering my Parents' Advice: "Do not fight and bear arms; get your education!"

It still rings a bell in my head: I was more than eager to learn the use of weapons in Syria and fight back against the Turkish dominance over the Armenians. Years later, after receiving my technical education in the United States—specifically in the rocket and aerospace field—it became clear to me that education will give an individual the necessary tools to carve their own future.

Picture from: *The Sun*, Lowell, Massachusetts, in the "People & Innovation" section "Education is More Important than Missiles"

Vahan V. Basmajian shown with the world's first oil-less, multi-fueled engine

Universal Education and Technology

One of the most important factors was to find channels that can be effectively utilized to get this message out to the public:

1. Fossil Fuels are of limited supply on the planet.

2. Use of fossil fuels has long-term negative impact on humans, plants, and life in general.

3. We must find new sources of clean, renewable energy and replace fossil fuels.

4. It is imperative to develop awareness about America's energy independence through educational institutions.

To highlight the importance of the above goals, I found great interest among the heads of states who could participate in a conference at MIT and get an orientation on the energy situation. The State Department of Education sent its respective leaders, who were willing to bring changes in high school programs to achieve the above goals. There is no doubt that it did. Since then, many schools have come up with a program that they call Energy, Power, and Transportation Technology. As President of Megatech Corporation, I took the company in the same direction the the leaders and professors at MIT had the vision to prepare us for.

It was very clear to me that I should direct the resources of Megatech in developing the proper curriculum, design new engines, and develop a geothermal heat pump. The latter one won the Invention of the Year Award from the Society of Professional Engineers!

for innovative use of
engineering principles and materials,
improved function and savings in use and
benefit to the national economy

1986 Small Company Category
**Geopump
Energy System**
Megatech Corporation

The world's first oil-less transparent engine that could run on any liquid or gaseous fuel

This system uses the earth as a source of energy

Megatech Corporation conducted extensive research in developing the geothermal heat pump, which proved this technology to be viable. A new building was constructed and technicians were hired to start the production. No doubt, this created the new jobs in the alternative energy industry. Certainly, the US Department of Energy New England (offices in Boston) gave us the award for this innovation, followed by a visit from state energy office director, Mr. Joe Fitzpatrick.

The price of oil was climbing. The Geopump trademark became a very popular word among all interested parties, including the Democratic Governor of Massachusetts, then Governor, Ed King. Most graciously, he accepted my invitation for the first opening ceremonies and installation site in Massachusetts.

The Boston Globe

TUESDAY, JULY 5, 1983

BUSINESS (EXTRA)

Reprinted Courtesy of The Boston Globe.

New energy firms rely on earth as a partner

By Fred Brodie
Contributing Reporter

Patrons relaxing in the Wakefield Colonial Hilton's pub probably aren't aware that the room's winter heat and summer air conditioning come from a hole in the ground.

A Woburn mechanical engraving firm and a nearby flute manufacturing concern also rely on the earth for heating and cooling. All three say they are saving money.

And all are using technology that has been around since the turn of the century, but is just now being fine-tuned into a system that can help larger energy consumers cut their bills substantially under the right circumstances.

Heat pumps are commonly used in air conditioners, freezers and water coolers. Now, researchers see "earth-coupled" heat pumps, which take advantage of the ground's constant temperature, as one answer to the high price of comfort. The technology is coming fast – and so are the budding entrepreneurs.

An estimated 20,000 earth heat pumps have been installed in US homes and businesses in the last five years, with an equal number in both Canada and Sweden over the same period. Together the three countries should install 20,000 more next year alone, says one engineer.

With the market has come the money.

"Four or five years ago, you could count all the manufacturers on one hand," said Robert Weaver, program coordinator at the energy technology extension of Oklahoma State University, home of the nation's largest earth heat pump research operation.

Vahan Basmajian, president of Megatech Corp. in Billerica, with his Geopump.
PHOTO BY JIM WILSON

From the *Boston Globe's*, "Business Extra" Section, July 5, 1983

Expanding My Horizons Through American Technology and Freedom

After escaping the Syria Army in Aleppo, my feelings toward America grew deeper and stronger than anything else. I found mutual respect and open-minded individuals that gave me both motivation and mentorship. To succeed, I realized that Middle East oil countries, combined with other OPEC countries, created a new "weapon" against the economic growth of the Western countries. The solution was clear to me:

"Let's educate the students of today in technology to deter the OPEC countries from using oil as a manipulative tool against us."

Mr. Basmajian welcoming the guests and emphasizing the importance of the joint meeting on Energy and Power at MIT

From Missiles to New Visions: Solving Problems

Prior to starting Megatech Corporation in 1970, I was cleared for *secret* and *top secret* status to work on missile aerodynamics with certain corporations in the United States. In less than ten years after escaping the Syrian army, America was giving me the opportunities to exercise my freedom and progress toward goals that were not possible in Syria. The energy crisis of 1973 motivated me to call upon my professors at MIT to give an overview of America's energy problems to educators. Invitations were sent out to approximately twenty key state departments of education directors, who attended the seminars. I have deep appreciation for both professors who accepted my vision to bring energy education programs to our public schools. Dr. Eugene Covert played a key role in shaping and mentoring me during the years of my graduate studies at MIT. His guidance and advice continued for the following twenty years and contributed in improving America's technical education in Energy and Power programs. He helped me start Megatech Corporation and joined the Board of Directors for many years. He wiped out from my mind any doubts that a Syrian-born Armenian could achieve the technical standards and launch a business dedicated to "free America" from the jaws of OPEC nations.

Dr. Covert, Chairman of the Curriculum Committee at M.I.T. and formerly U.S.A.F. Chief Scientist warns about the unwise consumption of fuel and points out how complicated it is to develop alternate sources and supplies of energy.

Working Toward Solutions to America's Energy Independence

Now that I was highly motivated to find solutions to America's energy problems, it became clear to me that the best way is to have dual approaches to solving problems.

1. Direct the company product line toward educating the American youth in learning alternative fuels and introduce new programs to all schools (see patents list).

2. Use my technical background to invent new products and systems that can replace the use of oil/gas in heating and cooling of a building. As a result of our efforts, Dr. Charles Haldeman and I received the "Invention of the Year" award from the Society of Professional Engineers in the US in 1985.

The great advantage of using the geothermal energy of the earth is obvious: it is controlled by us, and it is non-carbon based, available, and free—as is the solar energy radiating from the sun. The supply is available to all nations and will last billions of years.

Installation Ceremonies of the First Geothermal Heat Pump in Massachusetts, Supported by Governor Ed King (D)

The urgency of finding solutions toward America's energy independence gained further recognition by Gov. Ed King, who recognized the importance of innovative small companies in Massachusetts. He was willing to give his support for young entrepreneurs who were willing to take risk with higher rewards.

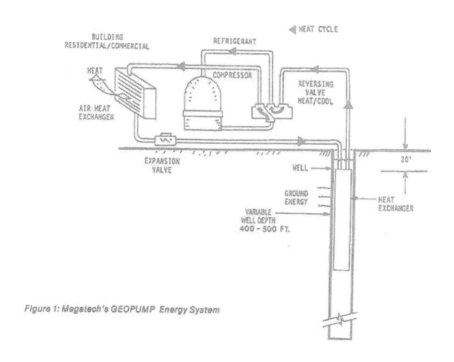

Figure 1: Megatech's GEOPUMP Energy System

Gov. Ed King during the dedication ceremonies of the Geopump Energy System

Vahan presenting the Geopump Energy System

EDWARD J. KING
Governor

Margaret N. St.Clair
Secretary

The Commonwealth of Massachusetts

Executive Office of Energy Resources

73 Tremont Street

Boston, Massachusetts 02108

(617) 727-4732

November 23, 1981

Vahan Basmajian, President
Megatech Corporation
29 Cook Street
Billerica, Massachusetts

RECEIVED DEC 14 1981

Dear Mr. Basmajian:

I was most pleased to be included in the dedication of the first Geopump Energy System. It was a very pleasant and informative morning.

I know full well that this innovation will contribute substantially to an alleviation of the energy crunch, not only in Massachusetts, but throughout the entire country. It is with particular delight that I envision a new energy related high technology industry to be located in the Commonwealth.

The Governor has asked me to send along the enclosed pens for your daughter and her friend. Unfortunately he did not have any with him this morning.

With warm personal regards and my best wishes for every possible success.

Sincerely,

Margaret N. St.Clair
Secretary

MSt.C/ev

enclosure

15. Trade Missions

Governor William F. Weld   &   Vahan V. Basmajian, CEO
Commonwealth of Massachusetts   Megatech Corporation

TRADE MISSION TO S. AFRICA

I was more than happy to respond to the invitations of subsequent governors to go on trade missions. We all had mutual interests where any governor, either Democrat or Republican, had to promote the Commonwealth's growing economy and highlight its universities. Foreign students coming to Massachusetts were bringing along brain power and funds to improve themselves and others who could benefit from the technological resources in Massachusetts. The infusions of immigrants who enter the United States with good intents, get educated, and follow the American laws were more than welcome!

I was very fortunate that Gov. "Bill" Weld took a group of selected people to promote the above goals to Brazil, Argentina, Chile, and South Africa.

The trade missions were very successful for me—and for Megatech. As an immigrant to the United States, I felt a strong bond to the countries visited: knowing very well that their needs were in line with mine and with Megatech.

Special Thanks to Governor Paul Cellucci

Gov. Paul Cellucci is one of the most special governors that I have ever met. In the news-media, I read about him: how friendly he is and how well he wants small, high-tech companies to succeed. He was more than happy to see emerging industries in Massachusetts be established and create jobs that will absorb the skilled workers of the state.

When I got the invitation to join him for a trade mission, it took me less than a minute to say, "Yes!" The trade mission to Mexico and then to Canada was most beneficial to all parties concerned. There were appointments made for me to see the Education Ministry Heads and Consultants in regard to assisting the Mexican government in obtaining the best available automotive technical lab (equipment from Massachusetts). I was totally surprised when the governor asked for a copy of Megatech's catalog and read it overnight. The next morning, he took the initiative to present Megatech. I was dead quiet: listening to his presentation in regard to Megatech's innovations, the founders, and my background. I was thinking, "What a true and sincere governor—to speak up as if he wants every dollar to come to the Commonwealth through Megatech." After the meeting, I turned around to the Trade Mission Coordinator. "I love this governor who acted just like a common man for the Commonwealth." We received contracts and orders from Mexico. We are still receiving more orders from Mexico.

The next Trade Mission was to Canada—with as much success. Now, I was seated next to him on the airplane and had a lot of chances to joke and have casual talks with him. I thought the governor was better than my Vice President in Marketing and Sales.

By now, he knew me very well, and we had mutual respect for each other. He sent me a letter (as shown here) to be on the Advisory for Renewable Energy Trust Fund Committee.

Governor	Vahan V. Basmajian
Argeo Paul Cellucci	President
Commonwealth of Massachusetts	Megatech Corporation

TRADE MISSION TO MEXICO

THE COMMONWEALTH OF MASSACHUSETTS
EXECUTIVE DEPARTMENT
STATE HOUSE • BOSTON 02133
(617) 727-3600

ARGEO PAUL CELLUCCI
GOVERNOR

JANE SWIFT
LIEUTENANT GOVERNOR

June 9, 2000

Vahan V. Basmajian
90 Deacon Haynes Road
Concord, Massachusetts 01742

Dear Mr. Basmajian:

Under the provisions of Massachusetts General Laws, Chapter 40J, Section 4E, I am pleased to appoint you a member of the Renewable Energy Trust Fund Advisory Committee. Please be advised that this appointment will be void unless the oath of office is taken within three months of the date of this letter.

Lieutenant Governor Swift and I appreciate your willingness to serve the Commonwealth in this capacity. Your experience and sound judgment will contribute substantially to the Committee throughout your tenure.

Congratulations on your appointment, and best wishes for success.

Sincerely,

Argeo Paul Cellucci

cc: Secretary of State
State Ethics Commission
Comptroller
Governor's Legislative Office
Massachusetts Technology Park Corporation

Trade Missions and Companies Visited Overseas

A. Trade Missions with Governor "Bill" Weld:

1) Brazil

2) Argentina

3) Chile

4) South Africa

B. Trade Missions with Governor Paul Cellucci:

1) Mexico

2) Canada

C. Author's Business Trips and Overseas Dealers Visiting Megatech:

1) Spain

2) Germany

3) Italy

4) Greece

5) England

6) Russia

7) Switzerland

8) Turkey

9) Lebanon

10) Egypt

11) Jordan

12) Iraq

13) Iran

14) Kuwait

15) Saudi Arabia

16) Oman

17) United Arab Emirates

18) Qatar

19) Philippines

20) Hong Kong

21) Formosa/Republic of China

22) Australia

23) India

24) Pakistan

25) Indonesia

26) Japan

27) South Korea

28) Yemen, and more....

Part III

Your Move

Technical Career Paths in Alternate Energy and Automotive Industries

President Obama

Looking into Megatech Trainers while visiting a college

Training equipment designed by Vahan V. Basmajian and Megatech staff.

It will be most beneficial if the teacher and guidance counselor share this section for its contents and technology involved before making a total commitment in this field. There is considerable information available for the instructor to use in a classroom: use it as a resource book.

Author's Intent

The author is very aware of the depth of the engineering and sciences involved in each of the topic areas of this book. There are many excellent textbooks available from many publishers. The Department of Energy, the Department of Labor, and countless organizations provide high quality information and data. What the author is striving to achieve with the publication is to connect the parents' involvement with the schools' instructors and their children. The author's view is one of integrating the family, their children, and education toward a career. This book gives supporting data and a road map for *all* parties involved to direct the person under training as to why they are better off to learn related sciences for that particular career/job.

America's energy independence can only be achieved through an educated country supporting good schools and guiding its children to meaningful careers and jobs.

There are vast amounts of information available in regard to:

- Alternative sources of energy for powering America

- Renewable energy options

- Supply and demand of energy from various sources

- What type of vehicles are available for an "educated" buyer of cars

- Starting in high schools, how these subjects can be taught

- What are the basic S̲cience, T̲echnology, E̲ngineering and M̲ath (STEM) principles that can be applied to:

    Energy—Power—Automotive Technology

- Parents and counselors knowing where the jobs are and providing this information to students

- Career Orientation: the student's road map toward future jobs and potentially available positions are offered as a tie-in and service; the students are shown how to achieve their goals with employable skills.

The author had vast experience in evaluating education in thirty countries and visiting all fifty states in the United States. Regardless of languages or the religious or political status of the governments, the common factor has been technology and sciences. All important concepts relating to science, technology, engineering, and math were common for all countries. These principles are available for all nations and students without discrimination. Science and technology stands on its own regardless of race, color, or nationality of the person living on this planet.

Overview
A Road Map to Success
Innovations and Jobs in the United States

A. Purpose of this Section

Throughout my life, I have learned some very basic principles that seem to work better for students and adults alike. The first is to establish goals. This section is intended to assist students and their parents to clarify their goals. Most high school graduates have no sense of direction in America's technological world. Parents are too busy to keep families together, keep their jobs, and survive. I came to the United States alone (without my parents), and I want to share with all youngsters what to look for and how to clarify their goals to achieve meaningful careers.

B. America's Energy Independence beyond Syria:

I escaped the Syrian Army when I was about eighteen years old, and I was very aware of Middle Eastern oil and OPEC policies and intents. As I developed my career path in the United States, my intent shifted toward "America's Energy Independence." Subsequent inventions in this field—and a list of patents I received—show clearly that America needs to take multiple approaches:

1. through engineering solutions with Alternate sources of energy,
2. through education and training of the next generation of students, and
3. with factual information for *all* citizens who care to read, be leaders, or get jobs in these industries.

This book leads the reader to be informed and make sound decisions with regard to developing new and emerging occupations and jobs in alternate energy and automotive industries.

1: Bridging the Gap by Applying S.T.E.M. to Automotive Technology

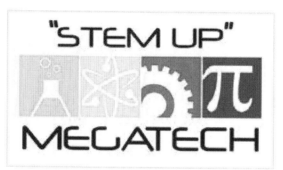

During the past century, the auto industry introduced new technologies in the areas of: engine design, combustion of fuels, transmissions, vehicle design, aerodynamics, and electronics and with many features that made the vehicles more efficient. The environmental aspect forced the auto industry to deal with the emissions of vehicles. As time progressed, hybrid vehicles came into existence, and new propulsion systems were introduced with electronic controls.

New vehicles required engineers and specialists that could integrate all the sciences to produce the new design. The common denominator, and the foundation, is based on <u>S</u>cience, <u>T</u>echnology, <u>E</u>ngineering, and <u>M</u>ath: "S.T.E.M." This is why this resource book ties in <u>S.T.E.M.</u> to energy-power and automotive technology.

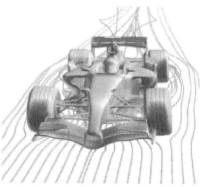

Heading toward auto industry careers

2: Structuring Career-Driven Programs

The traditional education programs in secondary schools taught science, physics, chemistry, math, and English for many decades. As technology evolved, the auto industry utilized new processes that required engineers to solve problems. However, solving problems required more math and modeling into computers.

This is why S.T.E.M. became the basis for many techs and engineers to build their careers. In today's world, all nations depend on certain versions of S.T.E.M. to build education and training programs for various careers. We will call S.T.E.M. a core/foundation for many evolving industries. Consider the graphics shown below. We must call it: 'S.T.E.M.-Up to automotive industry, S.T.E.M.-Up to construction industry, and more.

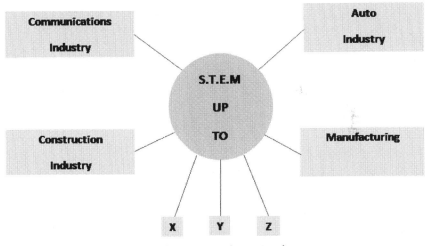

Industries – Enterprises – Services

The above Chart graphically shows that S.T.E.M.-Up programs can be applied to any sector of industry, services, or business.

The Department of Labor lists occupational titles for many industries and services. This section will allow the reader to explore all kinds of possibilities for his or her career path. Just name your choice, and you will find a long list of jobs/titles from the DOE and Department of Labor (DOL).

3: Why S.T.E.M. Applies to Automotive Technology

Build Your Own Career!

Today's vehicles incorporate many of the sciences and engineering principles that are taught in schools and colleges. A vehicle is an integrated science and a laboratory on wheels. You cover all of the S.T.E.M. subjects by using a vehicle to identify what it uses for fuel (energy), what kind of engine it has (energy conversion to power), what kind of transmission it uses (power transmission to wheels), the type of energy storage (batteries/fuel tank), and an unlimited number of examples correlating S.T.E.M. to energy-power and automotive technology.

S.T.E.M.-Up to Careers

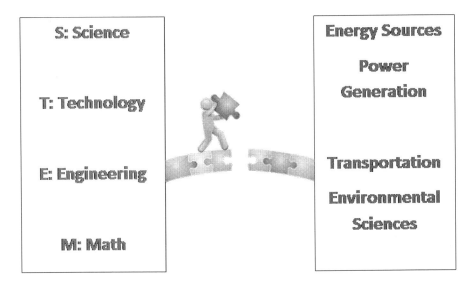

S: Science	Energy Sources
T: Technology	Power Generation
E: Engineering	Transportation
M: Math	Environmental Sciences

4: Applying S.T.E.M. to Automotive Technology

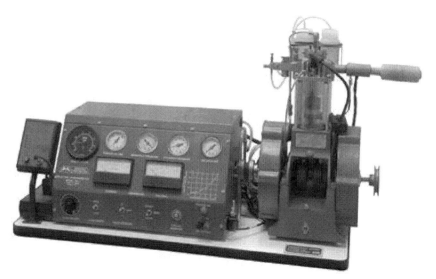

Megatech's Oil-Less 4-Cycle Engine

This 4-cycle oil-less, internal combustion engine is operable with alternative fuels and has a transparent cylinder which allows for full observation of combustion in the cylinder. The engine is capable of operating on any fuel and has variable compression ratio and variable spark timing. The engine shown is coupled to a 1HP Electric Dynamometer—mounted on a baseboard.

Just about all the technologies of S.T.E.M. principles can be shown live with the operation of this engine. The following presents a few activities and measurements:

1. Observe the combustion of fuel, type of fuel, energy content as measured with Btu's, gaseous/liquid fuel mixes, emissions, and many more

2. Engine torque, speed (RPM), horsepower as measured by the dynamometer is calculated using math. The force on the piston is the result of the surface area (π) X pressure (psi), which gives the actual force.

3. Electrical power generated from the dynamometer exemplifies the math required for OHM's law.

4. See how engineering principles were vastly used to solve many problems.

S.T.E.M.-Up to Automotive Technology
Hybrid Technology

Hybrid Engine Performance Trainer
Model: MEG007-HYB

This trainer is built from a hybrid model and converted into an engine performance trainer. It is complete with: running engine, transaxle, drivetrain, suspension, front brakes, dashboard electrical system, and computer.

Careers in the Auto Industry

Job opportunities are many in light of the fact that cars are changing constantly. Diesel buses, electric cars, hybrids, fuel cells, and others create a high demand for skilled technicians. Training programs are based on ASE/NATEF standards, which provide task lists for various levels. No doubt, any good ASE-certified tech knows all the basic math, sciences, and automotive engineering principles. A technician that has a good background in S.T.E.M. is destined to be on the highest levels of employability with good income.

5: Global View – Energy, Mass and Universal Laws

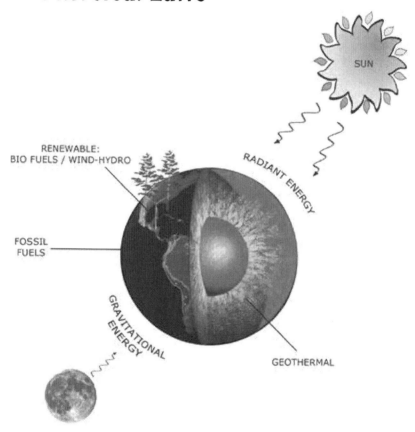

RENEWABLE: BIO FUELS / WIND-HYDRO

RADIANT ENERGY

SUN

FOSSIL FUELS

GRAVITATIONAL ENERGY

GEOTHERMAL

Energy can neither be created nor destroyed.

$$E = mc^2$$

Energy is very abundant everywhere: on Earth and in the universe. As a matter of fact, the entire universe is made of energy and mass. On Earth, it is possible to rank and classify energy as follows:

A. Earth-bound fossil fuels (carbon based)

B. Nuclear: Naturally found on Earth

C. Natural sources of energy (non-carbon based): Solar, geo-thermal, gravitational, wind, hydro, etc.

Now we can take a look into the estimated supplies of energy.

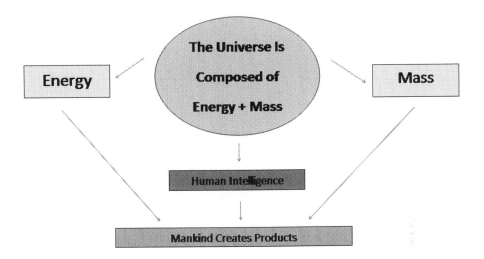

Useful interpretation of science, math, physics, chemistry, biology, and engineering principles combine the best of energy and mass to create:

1) useful products through raw materials (i.e. copper, iron, aluminum), combined with energy, to make cars and consumer products,

2) living quarters, buildings, construction materials for bridges, highways, space-conditioning equipment, etc.,

3) improved tools for manufacturing,

4) better energy conversion devices for power generation and distribution, and

5) hundreds of other examples you can see in daily life.

What is the Common Denominator?

Applying *S*ciences, *T*echnologies, *E*ngineering & *M*ath (S.T.E.M.)

Through *HUMAN INGENUITY*

6: Powering the Planet: Energy Sources, Supply, and Demand

Energy Sources:

As shown earlier, America's energy sources are categorized as:

1) Earthbound—such as fossil fuels (carbon based)

2) Nuclear—naturally found on Earth (non-carbon)

3) Natural sources (non-carbon)

   a. Hydro

   b. Wind

   c. Gravitational

   d. Geothermal

   e. Solar

   f. Tidal

There are many ways of converting these sources of energy into useful power. The most important factors have to do with: economics, installation location, cost of energy conversion system (payback period), environmental aspects, and consumer acceptance.

Energy Supply in the United States:

A. Fossil Fuels	Years
1. Gasoline	40–50
2. Natural Gas	100–150
3. Coal	150–200

B. Nuclear

    1. Uranium   **50**

    2. Fusion   **(Not Ready)**

C. Renewable and natural sources of energy (several billion years)

Energy Demand:

The economic growth of any nation is shown by its energy consumption. There is a direct correlation between economic growth vs. energy consumption. These are categorized by user sectors:

1) Transportation industry: cars, buses, airplanes, trucks, ocean liners, and other ground vehicles.

2) Residential: all home electricity for heating/cooling and operating household items.

3) Commercial: office building, shopping malls and businesses that need energy for lighting, heating, air conditioning, and many other items.

4) Industrial: American industry operating heavy manufacturing equipment and processing of materials that consume enormous energy/power.

U.S. energy consumption by sector, 1960 and 2010

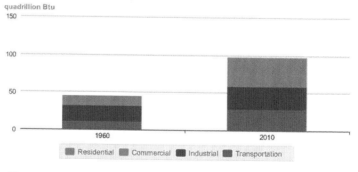

Source: U.S. Energy Information Administration, State Energy Data System 2010

Energy Consumption: What Type of Fuel?

Energy types, prices, emissions, and many other factors/regulations dictate how much is consumed in the United States. To make comparisons, all energy could be compared by the Btu's consumed in a year. The chart below shows that America is heavily dependent on fossil fuels.

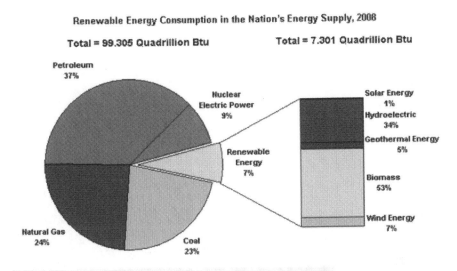

Renewable Energy Consumption in the Nation's Energy Supply, 2008

Source: Energy Information Administration, Office of Coal, Nuclear, Electric and Alternate Fuels

7: Energy Conversion Devices

The most common energy conversion device is the internal combustion engine, which is used with many vehicles. These are known as "gas engines" with sparked ignition. The diesel engine is known as a compression ignition.

The external combustion in power plants burning coal/oil/gas is all external combustion. The chart below shows various types of energy conversion devices that are designed to power America.

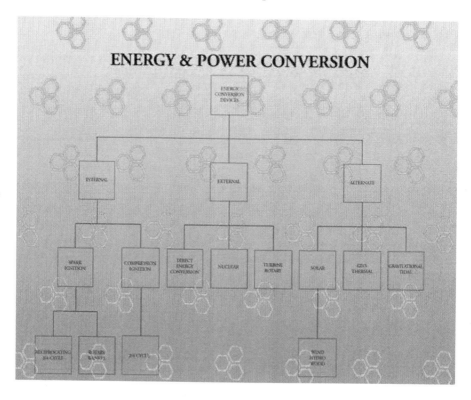

8: Energy & Power Transmission

Depending on what type of energy conversion device generates power, it must transmit to the point of use. For example, the automobile uses transmission to get the power to the wheels; a home's electrical power comes through conducting wires; and microwaves use electromagnetic waves to transmit power to whatever is being heated or cooked.

There are many more examples that can be listed by the reader; however, they can be categorized as shown below.

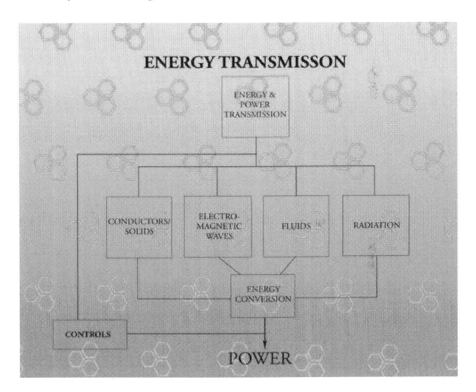

9: Energy Storage

Automobiles use batteries to start engines and power auxiliary equipment. Computers use a different type of energy storage: known as the lithium-ion battery. The Hoover Dam uses water behind its dam to power its turbines. There are many ways that energy is stored, and its application is dictated by the device in use. Below are the categories of energy storage systems that are widely used in America.

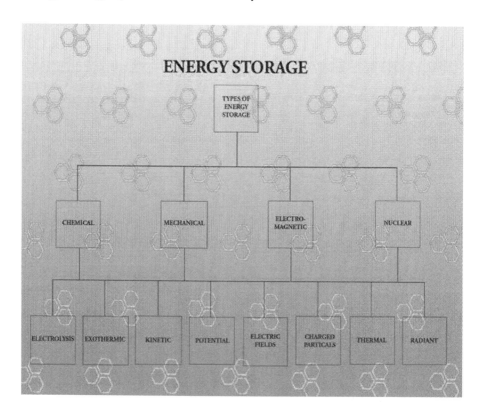

10: Transportation Systems for Ground Vehicles

Fuels: Energy content

The four sectors in the United States which consume most of the energy are recorded yearly. They are categorized into Residential, Commercial, Industrial, and Transportation. Because almost every consumer uses a vehicle for travel, it is clear that they purchase fossil fuels from the gas station. In search of new resources of energy (especially renewable), the following shows what it takes to produce power.

Power Production:

- **Coal accounts for 23% of the total energy consumed by the United States**

- **1000 megawatts (MW) uses 8000 tons of coal per day**

- **The above can be replaced with wind turbines (each at 5 MW output times (x) 200 units in a wind farm)**

- Solar PV installation requires 3000–4000 acres of land in the Southwest to produce the same 1000 MW from coal. There are millions of acres in the Southwest controlled by the US government.

How about the transportation industry?

There are over thirty million on-the-road/off-the-road buses/trucks that use diesel fuel. There are over one hundred fifty million cars that use gasoline and blends. The mixture, types, and prices vary in the United States. The one scientific way to know is to look at the chart below, which gives you the chemical formulae and the energy content in Btu's. Now you know the difference in the types of trucks and energy content. It is quite clear that hydrogen has the highest energy content. If the liquid form is used on cars/buses with specially designed tanks (not ready yet, except in gaseous state), then the range will be far better than gasoline and emission minor with air or nothing (zero) with oxygen.

Fuel	Empirical Formula	Molecular Weight	Density	Heat of Combustion (Btu/lb)
Hydrogen Gas	H_2	2	.00520 lb/ft³	53000
Ammonia Gas	NH_3	17	.0438 lb/ft³	8350
Propane Gas	C_3H_8	44	.116 lb/ft³	20600
Acetone	C_3H_6O	58	.179 gm/cc	13500
Benzene	C_6H_6	78	.879 gm/cc	18000
Ether	$C_4H_{10}O$	74	.714 gm/cc	16000
Carbon Heptane	C_7H_{16}	100	.684 gm/cc	20500
Carbon Hexane	C_2H_{14}	84	.659 gm/cc	20700
Ethyl Alcohol	C_2H_6O	46	.789 gm/cc	12300
Methyl Alcohol	CH_4O	32	.791 gm/cc	9350

Types of Vehicles:

The US Department of Energy has defined with clarity the several types of engines that power transport vehicles. It is best served as we quote from the DOE's website, as follows:

Electric Vehicles:

There are two types of electric vehicles currently in use: battery-operated electrics and hybrid electric vehicles, or HEVs. Battery-operated electrics run on electricity stored in batteries: electricity that ultimately comes from the generating plants that also provide our homes with electrical power. With HEVs, most electricity is produced by small onboard generating plants driven by internal combustion engines. HEVs can be designed to run on gasoline, diesel, or alternative fuels.

Battery-operated electric vehicles are sometimes referred to as "zero emission vehicles," because they do not directly pollute through tailpipe emissions, fuel evaporation, fuel refining, or fuel transport to service stations. A certain amount of pollution, however, is associated with the use of these vehicles. This comes from power plant emissions. Pollution levels from battery-operated electric vehicles remain extremely low even when these emissions are taken into account.

One reason this is true is that the generators and motors used in electric vehicles are much more efficient than the powertrains of internal combustion engines. The difference is such as to make it more efficient to burn an amount of fuel in a power plant to generate electricity for an electric vehicle than to burn it directly in a vehicle's internal combustion engine. Adding to the efficiency of electric vehicles is the technique of regenerative braking. This involves slowing and stopping a vehicle by absorbing its energy and converting it to electricity that may be returned to the vehicle's onboard battery. In a conventional vehicle, this energy is simply wasted as heat.

Of course, burning less fuel in going a certain distance does not necessarily make for less pollution. That depends on the efficiency of and emissions from the power plant providing the electricity. Over 95 percent of the fuel used to generate electrical power comes from within the United States in the form of: coal, natural gas, nuclear power, hydropower, and renewable energy sources.

Electric vehicles turn out to be more than 90 percent cleaner than that cleanest conventional gasoline-powered vehicle when the electricity running them comes from clean energy sources, such as: natural gas, nuclear power, hydropower, or renewable fuels.

Electric vehicles remain cleaner than comparable gasoline-powered vehicles even when the electricity they use derives from polluting fuels like coal. The reasons are their high-efficiency electric powertrains and the fact that modern coal-burning generating plants produce electricity more efficiently and with fewer emissions than they did in the past.

The environmental benefits from using battery-operated electric vehicles promise to increase with time. That's because electric generation continues getting cleaner as older, dirtier generating plants are being taken out of service and replaced with newer, less polluting ones, and as pollution-free solar or wind generators come online.

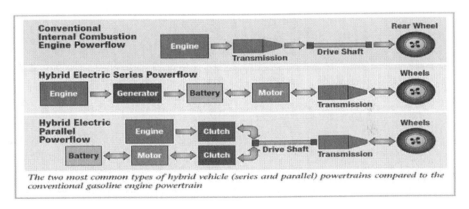

The two most common types of hybrid vehicle (series and parallel) powertrains compared to the conventional gasoline engine powertrain

Operation of HEVs:

Much development work has gone into HEVs, which provide the efficiency advantages of electric drive-trains without burdening vehicles with the large, heavy battery packs found in battery-operated electrics. HEVs basically consist of an internal combustion engine, a generator to turn the energy developed by the engine into electricity, and an electric motor to propel the vehicle. Hybrids also include a relatively small battery pack to store energy recovered through regenerative braking and to provide extra power beyond what the generator can produce on its own when the vehicle must accelerate quickly.

Current HEVs produce very low emissions because of their electric powertrains and their highly efficient internal combustion engines. The engines in conventional vehicles are relatively inefficient under average driving conditions, because they are designed for peak-demand situations, which occur when a vehicle is accelerating or climbing up a steep hill. By contrast, the fuel-burning engines that run generators in HEVs

MEG-MG1/MG2: Hybrid Drive Cutaway

are tailored to efficiently meet the average power requirements of the vehicles, since onboard batteries handle surge power requirements.

Driving an electric vehicle is very similar to driving a gasoline-fueled vehicle. Well-designed electrics can travel at the same speeds as conventional vehicles and provide similar performance capabilities. However, the engines of some HEVs are designed to shut off automatically when the vehicle is braking or stopped at a red light, which can be a little disconcerting to drivers at first. The driving ranges of battery-operated electric vehicles typically vary from fifty to 130 miles—depending on a vehicle's weight, its design features, and the type of battery it uses. By contrast, some HEVs being produced today have driving ranges that approximately double the three-hundred-mile range of conventional vehicles.

What battery-operated vehicles give up in range, they return in re-fueling convenience. Drivers can refuel a battery-operated vehicle by simply plugging it into a special recharging outlet at home. The recharging time depends on: the voltage of the recharging station, the ambient air temperature, the size and type of the battery pack, and the remaining electrical energy in storage. Typically, the process takes several hours, but batteries are being developed that can be recharged more quickly. The cost of fully recharging a battery pack varies with the rates charged by local utility companies, but generally, it is considerably less than the cost of an equivalent amount of gasoline.

Electric vehicles are significantly more expensive to purchase than comparable conventional vehicles. An additional expense with battery-operated vehicles involves replacing the vehicle's batteries every few years.

Diesel Engines:

Some passenger cars utilize diesel engines so that they get higher fuel efficiency/mileage. However, the percentage is far less than gasoline. The trucking industry has been using diesels for a long time—including construction and farming machinery. Diesels are workhorse engines, powering heavy-duty trucks, buses, tractors, and trains—not to mention large ships, bulldozers, cranes, and other construction equipment. Like a gasoline engine, a diesel is an internal combustion engine that converts chemical energy in fuel to mechanical energy that moves pistons up and down inside enclosed spaces, called cylinders. The pistons are connected to the engine's crankshaft, which changes their linear motion into the rotary motion needed to propel the vehicle's wheels. Training programs are available from Megatech Corporation, as shown below.

MEG320: Diesel Engine Performance Trainer

Diesel Fuel Injection:

Air heats up when it's compressed. This fact led German engineer, Rudolf Diesel, to theorize that fuel could be made to ignite spontaneously if the air inside an engine's cylinders became hot enough through compression. Part of the reason is that compressing air concentrates fuel-burning oxygen. A fuel that has high energy content per gallon, like diesel fuel, should be able to react with most of the concentrated oxygen to deliver more punch per explosion, if it were injected into an engine's cylinders at exactly the right time. As a result, the basic concept of the four-stroke diesel engine has remained virtually unchanged for over one hundred years.

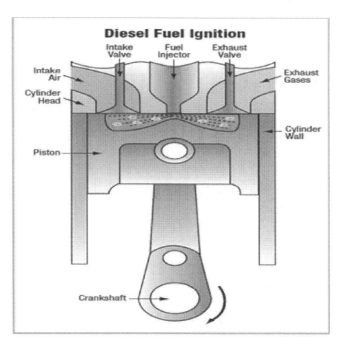

The first stroke involves drawing air into a cylinder as the piston creates space for it by moving away from the intake valve. The piston's subsequent upward swing then compresses the air, heating it at the same time. Next, fuel is injected under high pressure as the piston approaches the top of its compressions stroke, igniting spontaneously as it contacts the heated air. The hot combustion gases expand, driving the piston downward in what's called the power stroke. During its return swing, the piston pushes spent gases from the cylinder, and the cycle begins again with an intake of fresh air.

In the modern direct-injection diesel engine, fuel combustion is confined to a specially shaped region within the head of each piston. There, diesel fuel ignites spontaneously, in a carefully controlled manner. Old-style, indirect–injection diesels were not capable of this precision. As a result, fuel efficiency suffered, and emissions soared.

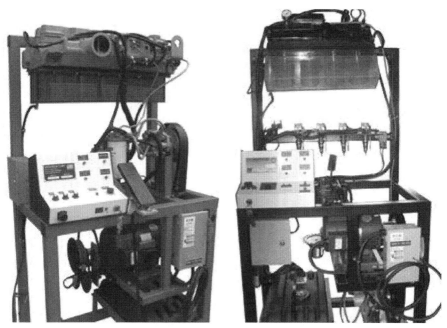

Megatech manufactured MEG550DCR & MEG550D Cummins Diesel Trainer: Electronically Controlled Common Rail & Power Stroke

Today's diesels inject fuel directly into an engine's cylinders using tiny computers to deliver precisely the right amount of fuel the instant it is needed. All functions in a modern diesel engine are controlled by an electronic control module that communicates with an elaborate array of sensors placed at strategic locations throughout the engine to monitor everything from engine speed to coolant and oil temperatures and even piston position. Tight electronic control means that fuel burns more thoroughly, delivering more power, greater fuel economy, and fewer emissions than yesterday's diesel engines could achieve.

Modern direct-injection diesel engines produce low amounts of carbon dioxide, carbon monoxide, and unburned hydrocarbons. Emissions of reactive nitrogen compounds (commonly spoken of as NOx) and particulate matter (PM) have been reduced by over 90 percent since 1980. Nevertheless, NOx and PM emissions remain at relatively high levels. NOx contributes to acid rain and smog, while adverse health effects have been associated with exposures to high PM amounts.

Diesel engines are already more efficient than gasoline engines (45 percent versus 30 percent), and further advances are possible (to 55–63 percent). The widespread use of diesel engines—particularly in trucks, vans, and sport utility vehicles—promises to substantially reduce consumption due to better mileage. The stumbling block to reaching this goal, however, remains NOx and PM emissions. Unfortunately, increasing diesel efficiency does not necessarily make these emissions go away.

What is Biodiesel?

The diesel engines that power most trucks and buses are not only highly efficient power plants; they are also very versatile in the fuels they can use. Rudolf Diesel first conceived of the engine that now bears his name as running on powdered coal. A ruinous engine explosion taught him to value liquid fuels. He subsequently hit on the idea of using vegetable oil. The engine that he demonstrated at the World Exhibition in Paris in 1900 ran on oil extracted from peanuts.

Nearly a century of reliance on dwindling petroleum reserves has taught us the wisdom of looking to Nature's bounty for our fuels—as Rudolf Diesel once did. Biofuels, such as biodiesel and bioethanol, are good for the environment, because they add fewer emissions to the atmosphere than petroleum-based fuels. Biofuels are also made from plant materials, which are available in inexhaustible supply. The energy content of plants comes from the sun through the natural process of photosynthesis.

Biodiesel Recycles Carbon Dioxide

CO_2

Biodiesel

Curtsey: DOE

That energy content persists even when plants are processed into other materials. Biodiesel is a biodegradable and nontoxic diesel fuel substitute that can be used in late-model (after 1992) diesel engines without any need to modify the engines beforehand. Biodiesel is actually good for diesel engines. It lubricates better than petroleum-based diesel fuel and has excellent solvent properties. Conventional diesel fuel can leave deposits inside fuel lines, storage tanks, and fuel delivery systems over time. Biodiesel dissolves this sediment while adding no deposits of its own, resulting in cleaner, more trouble-free fuel handling systems once fuel filters clogged with diesel sediments have been replaced after the switch to biodiesel has been made. Use of 100 percent biodiesel fuel does reduce the fuel economy and power of diesel engines by 10 percent. This means that 1.1 gallons of biodiesel are equivalent to one gallon of conventional diesel fuel. Although both biodiesel and conventional diesel fuel tend to gel or freeze in cold weather, biodiesel switches from the liquid stated at higher temperatures than petroleum-based diesel fuel.

Diesel engines can use alternate fuels, much like CNG and natural gas. Megatech Corp in MA manufactures Test Stands with dynamometers to test various fuels and train techs in schools. Biodiesel can easily be used with these types of setups.

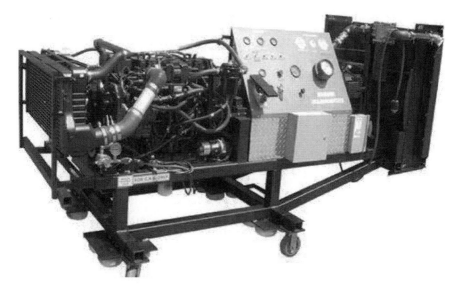

Megatech MEG330-CNG: Alternative Fuels Engine Test Stand w/ Closed Loop Dynamometer

Biodiesel is not a type of vegetable oil. Although diesel engines will run on various vegetable oils, prolonged use of these fuels can cause engine deposits that eventually lead to engine failures. These problems can be avoided, however, by modifying the oil-based feedstock materials. A process called trans-esterification chemically alters organically derived oils in forming biodiesel fuel.

Biodiesel is safe to handle and transport because: it is as biodegradable as sugar, ten times less toxic than table salt, and burns at a relatively high temperature. Biodiesel actually degrades about four times faster than petroleum-based diesel fuel when accidentally released into the environment.

Because it is physically similar to petroleum-based diesel fuel, bio-diesel can be blended with diesel fuel in any proportion. Many federal and state fleet vehicles now use biodiesel blends in their diesel engines. The most common blend is a mixture consisting of 20 percent biodiesel and 80 percent petroleum diesel, called B20. The motive for blending the fuels is to gain some of the advantages of biodiesel while avoiding higher costs. Biodiesel is currently higher in price than conventional diesel fuel.

Biodiesel Emissions:

The production and use of biodiesel creates 78 percent less carbon dioxide emissions than conventional diesel fuel. Carbon dioxide is a greenhouse gas that contributes to global warming by preventing some of the sun's radiations from escaping the Earth. Burning biodiesel fuel also effectively eliminates sulfur oxide and sulfate emissions, which are major contributors to acid rain. That's because, unlike petroleum-based diesel fuel, biodiesel is free of sulfur impurities. Combustion of biodiesel additionally provides a 56 percent reduction in hydro-carbon emissions and yields significant reductions in carbon monoxide and soot particles compared to petroleum-based diesel fuel. Also, biodiesel can reduce the carcinogenic properties of diesel fuel by 94 percent.

2- & 4-Cycle Gas Engines:

There are over 150 million cars in the United States that use 4-cycle gas engines, followed by 2-cycle engines. The passenger cars depend on 4-cycle, because 2-cycle engines require pre- mixing of oil with fuel. However, 2-cycle engines weigh less; this means they are best for chain saws and outboard motors.

The emissions from 2-cycle engines are higher than 4-cycle engines due to the unburned oil from the exhaust. In either case, dynamometers can measure the horsepower and exhaust gas analyzer can show the emissions. The most important aspects and parameters that affect horsepower and emissions are shown below:

4-Cycle Engine Performance

The most important factors that affect engine performance and emissions are:

1. the type of fuel used: gas, diesel, methanol, etc.,

2. fuel/air mixture ratio,

3. ignition timing,

4. compression ratio, and

5. air temperature and pressure.

Engine Power vs. Emissions

• Engine power is measured by a dynamometer (DYNO).

• DYNOs come with gauges and readouts of torque, RPM, engine temperature, etc.

• DYNO is a device that absorbs power in the form of friction (Hydraulics) or electricity.

• Electric DYNOs are more accurate and the power is *not* wasted in heat.

• Electric DYNOs can be used as starters/generators.

The horsepower of an engine is one factor that characterizes car choice for the consumer. The next factor is the torque that the engine is rated at by the manufacturer. The formula below shows how the horsepower is measured and calculated with Megatech's oil-less engine.

2-/4-cycle engines: IC Engine Power Output

- 2-/4-cycle engines use similar fuels, except 2-cycle requires pre-mixing of oil with fuel.

- Power output of 2-cycle (gas or diesel) engines per pound of weight is higher than 4-cycle.

- Torque-speed curves of 2-cycle and 4-cycle are very different: 2-cycle runs at higher RPM, but at a lower torque. The horsepower is measured the same way for either type of engine

  Torque = Force x Radius

Where force is applied by the connecting rod to the crankshaft journal

$$\text{HP (horsepower)} = \frac{1}{63{,}030} \times \text{RPM} \times \text{Torque}$$

Where Torque is measured in in-lbs

A dynamometer is designed to absorb the power output of an engine. This can be done with a friction device (just like a car brake), hydraulically (water/oil pump), or magnetically/electrically: just as a starter of an automobile. The principle methods used for Megatech electrical dynos are shown here.

How a DYNO can be used as a starter:

This figure shows the DYNO as a motor. STATOR is the outer casing. ROTOR is the shaft that rotates inside the casing. Armature and brushes provide currents and energize the motor.

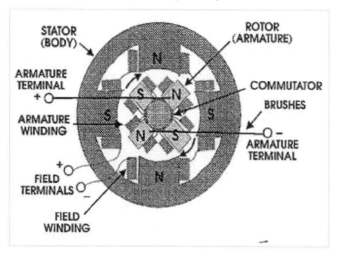

AS A DYNO: An electrical current is supplied to the field coils in the stator. A car battery is used to provide the current. A variable resistor is used to change the current, which affects the magnetic fields. The armature cuts the magnetic lines to absorb power. This resistance produces power output, torque, and RPM readings.

This is the function of a DYNO.

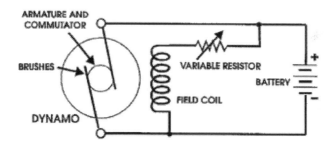

11: Alternate Sources of Power

A. Hydro Power

The transportation industry depends heavily on gas/diesel fuels that cause most of the emissions. Now, hybrid and electric cars are manufactured to lower the use of fossil fuels. Certainly, electric vehicles seem to have zero emissions, but the electricity is generated from an energy source. In this section, several of these sources are discussed, including how electrical power is generated from hydro-plants, solar power, wind turbines, geothermal sources, and fuel cells. It is vital to realize that when producing electricity from coal/oil/gas, there are considerable carbon emissions that cause global warming. Yet, hydro-plants have no such problem.

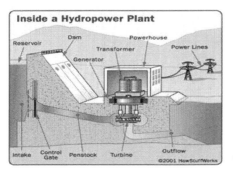 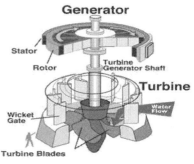

There are many turbine designs depending on the source of water: is it a river or a dam? How much/fast does the river flow, or how high is the dam? The hydro-power plants use the same principles as shown below:

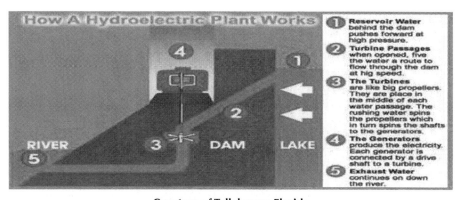

Courtesy of Tallahassee Florida

Courtesy of City of Tallahassee, Florida

Also, a simple formula can reveal the theoretical power that could be available from the following formula:

Theoretical HP (THP) = QVH/11.81 [horsepower]

Where: Q= Flow of water in cu.ft./sec.

H= Height of water level in ft.

11.8 = A constant

The critical advantage of a dam is the fact that it recycles itself through rain.

The "amount" of electricity produced is directly dependent on:

- Height of the water level (Inlet Pressure)
- Amount of water discharge (Mass rate of flow)
- Turbine design
- Generator

Renewable energy process:

- Discharge goes into oceans.
- Solar Energy evaporates water to rain clouds.
- Rain brings down the water back to the reservoir.

THE ABOVE PROCESS CREATES CLEAN ENERGY: NON-OPEC & NON-CARBON ENERGY!

Hydro generators work in the same manner as any generator: regardless of the dam's height or the river's flow rate.

Megatech Corporation in MA manufactures small hydro generators that can be set up in a training center so the student can see how the process works.

POTENTIAL ENERGY = mass of water x height of water level

- The pressure at the bottom of the reservoir is converted to electricity through Faraday's Law of Induction.

- Any conductor (wire loop) that rotates in a magnetic force field will produce voltage (electrical pressure).

- A light bulb is a "load:" when connected to the end of wire, the electrical loop is complete.

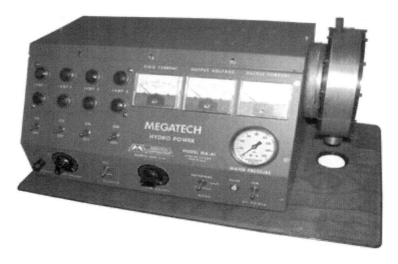

Megatech MEGWA1: Hydroelectric Generator

Hydro Generator

1. Simple wire loop rotating inside a magnet is the basis of an armature.

2. Permanent Magnet: It has an N + S pole.

3. Magnetic strength is fixed. It's called, "stator."

When an electric car is plugged into the home outlet for overnight charging, it is storing the energy in its batteries. Car batteries provide the power for starting engines or driving electric cars. The power from 12V DC batteries is measured by:

$$Pwatts = A \times V$$

Where: A = Amps
          V = Volts

In hydro-plants, we measure the power output in watts. Shown below are the important factors that are considered in understanding the basic principles of hydropower:

a) The number of wires can be increased in an armature.

b) Magnetic strength can be increased by electrical wires looped around the ends of the magnets; we call these electromagnets.

c) Water flow rates can be controlled for a given height of a reservoir: the head pressure.

*Ampere's Law: Physicist Biot-Savart Law states that as you increase the current in coils, the magnetic field strength increases.

WORK = Force x Distance (A motor lifting 550lb x 1ft high)

POWER = Force x Distance / Time (sec)

1 HP = 550 lb-ft/sec

1 HP = 750 watts

Power in Watts = Volts x Amps

Turbines

There are many designs of turbines: depending on the source of water. The two major designs are shown here.

Reaction Turbine:

This is one that is completely submerged in the water that flows down into it.

- Reaction turbines are best suited for high-pressure, low-flow rates.

- Hoover Dam is six times higher than Niagara Falls. The higher pressure could crack/damage the turbines. This is why impulse turbines are better suited with higher pressure dams.

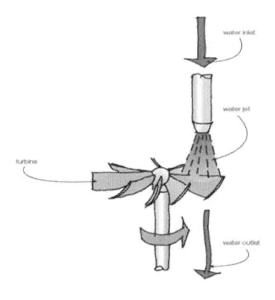

Impulse Turbine:

This turbine converts the kinetic energy of the water striking the blades of the turbine. This is similar to when the nozzle of a garden hose strikes the blades of a water wheel.

Power plants operate below their full capacity at night and maximum at daylight. They are a good available source for electric cars, because power companies are considering lowering rates for nighttime uses of power. This kind of policy usually benefits both parties: the power companies and the electric car owners.

B. Solar Photovoltaic Energy

Solar energy is considered a viable, reliable source and does NOT depend on imports or have the environmental impact of fossil fuels. The photovoltaic (PV) panels and cells are seen in use on radios, watches, calculators, and huge sites where megawatts of power are generated for distribution through power companies.

The PV panels collect the solar waves through specially manufactured semiconductors as shown below to produce direct current (DC) power.

Unlimited Energy in the form of Heat (Fusion) and Radiant
135 watts/m²(w/m²)

Sunlight has wavelengths, measured in nanometers.

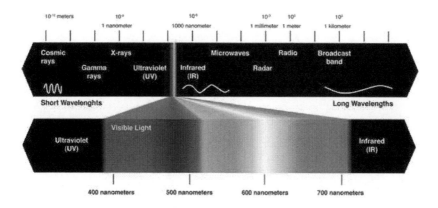

Photovoltaic Cells:

- They are made of silicon crystals, common on Earth.

- Cells have p type, positive layer of doped crystal with boron and phosphorous.

- N type is negative layer of silicon.

- The two layers form a semiconductor p-n junction.

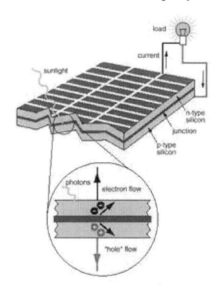

The sunlight is converted into useful power by using either direct, as DC power, or using invertors that can be converted to alternating current (AC) power.

The direct use of DC power is shown below: where a light bulb is connected to the semiconductors. There is a direct correlation between the resistance of the bulb, current, and the voltage. This correlation is expressed by OHM's Law:

$$I = E/R$$

This simple relationship shows that the bulb's resistance will limit the current going through it, just like a water valve cutting off water flow in a pipe.

Solar Power Generation

- Silicon cells can be made very small for watches, etc. They are known as microgenerators.

- Larger power is produced by many cells forming a solar panel.

- More power is generated through solar arrays.

Photovoltaic Operation:

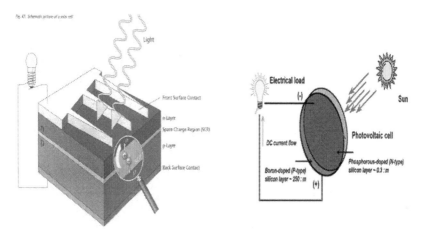

Another use of solar energy is for transportation purposes. As stated earlier, the sunlight energy can be stored in batteries and then used for various applications. The source of energy is the battery that can power a DC motor which can propel a golf cart. Some golf carts have installed PV panels and get their energy from the sun (free to all).

Anytime solar energy is converted into another application/form of energy, there is a loss in the process. This is no different than a gasoline engine where friction in the engine causes loss of power. This process is shown below.

Solar Energy and Power

- Solar energy can be measured by KW-Hrs.

- The sun sends out to Earth about 135 w/m².

- About one-third is lost in air.

- The amount of total energy on Earth is 745 quadrillion KW-Hrs.

- Solar panels put out current at a certain voltage. Power = Volts x Amps.

Solar Power vs. Efficiency

- Solar cells max efficiency is 25 percent.

- Solar cells function at a wide range of sunlight, except at very low light levels.

- Note the knee of each curve at high and medium light levels.

- Light intensity drops by the "Inverse Square Low." Double the distance from the source, you get one-fourth the light intensity.

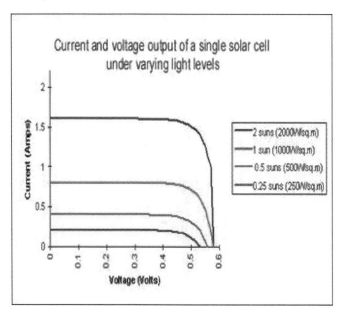

C. Wind Power

Wind power has been utilized for centuries, especially in sailing across the oceans. Over two thousand years ago, the Egyptian pharaohs had sailing boats that were found preserved near their tombs. Columbus crossed the Atlantic Ocean and discovered America. Sailboats are used for both pleasure and powering boats in many forms and shapes. The wind was used by many European farmers centuries ago who found it helpful in pumping water by "windmills." Today's wind turbines can be found in many parts of the United States and help to generate sufficient power in lighting up thousands of homes. The energy is free and has no carbon when it comes to generating electricity. Best of all, the power generated is three times the wind velocity (also known as the third power) as shown below.

- Wind turbines fall into two categories: low and high.

- Large diameter rotors are designed for low wind speeds.

- High wind speeds require lesser sizes.

- In both cases, gearing up/down is required to match the generator's performance.

- Wind power is proportional to the third degree of wind speed and velocity, where:

  - P = wind stream power

  - V = wind stream velocity

  - $P \sim V^3$

- If you double wind speed, it produces eight times the power.

The design of wind turbines is similar to aircraft wings. The cross-section of the wind "blades" is similar to the airfoil design of an aircraft's wing section. The aerodynamics play a key role in increasing the efficiency of the wind turbine blades, as well as size, number of blades, and if it is designed for high-speed wind/rotation. The design can be very complex: a simple calculation will show how many factors must be considered in a wind turbine:

- Wind Turbine designs have emerged over a period of time, because efficiency is a serious matter.

- The best way is to understand how designers have come up with a formula known as the *tip ratio*:

$$T = V_t / V_{wind}$$
V_t = Velocity at tip of turbine
V_w = Velocity of wind
V_t = 0.0319 x RPM

- High-efficiency turbines work best at ratios of ten

Horizontal Axis Wind Turbine

- The design is identical to an airplane wing. It generates forces that are similar to a 747 airplane wing, where each turbine blade could reach fifty feet in length.

- Wind Turbines are up to one hundred feet in diameter and produce five megawatts of power.

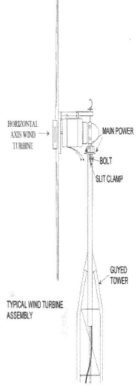

HORIZONTAL AXIS WIND TURBINE

MAIN POWER

BOLT

SLIT CLAMP

GUYED TOWER

TYPICAL WIND TURBINE ASSEMBLY

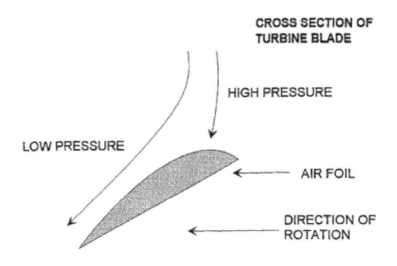

All wind turbines convert the energy of the wind into useful power. The system consists of wind turbines, a generator, invertor, batteries, and a vertical post to hold the turbine. There are many designs which are based on either a horizontal axis or vertical axis design. The vertical axis design can be held up against high-speed wind. This is better for small to medium size and allows the generator to be mounted on the ground. Certainly, this allows the maintenance crews to repair and replace them with ease—compared to the horizontal axis turbines. Megatech Corporation of Massachusetts manufactures equipment where the student could vary the number of blades and pitch angle and introduce new ideas.

Vertical Axis Wind Turbine

- Advantage of a vertical axis is that the generator can be located conveniently at the lower/ground level.

- It can stand up to high, gusty winds.

- It is easy to maintain.

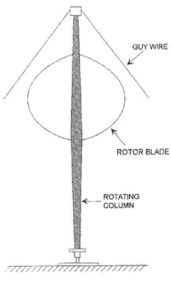

VERTICAL-AXIS TURBINE

Wind Power

The student can see how wind power is converted into electricity.

D. Geothermal Power

The earth's core is made of lava. This energy is available to everyone around the world, varying only when it reaches the crust of the world. The supply is unlimited (three to five billion years). Just like solar energy, it needs to be converted into useful power. There are two categories of geothermal wells. The first one spews out steam and hot water: just as the geysers do in Yellowstone. The second approach is to inject water into the hot rocks of the earth and have steam come up from a second well drilled several thousand feet into the crust. In both cases, what is most important is that we are obtaining energy from the earth.

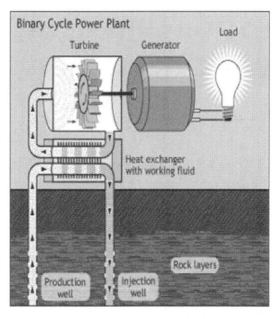

Geothermal plants operate just like coal-fired, steam-powered plants. In this case, steam turbines are the preferred approach, because they are more efficient and have been built for the past century. Overall, geothermal energy offers another option to build power stations without burning fossil fuels. As an example, a coal-burning power station that produces one thousand megawatts of power for half a million homes burns approximately eight thousand tons of coal a day. The carbon emissions cause global warming; whereas, the geothermal energy has much less environmental impact, due to its mineral residue and the thermal emissions from the earth.

Coal Power Plant

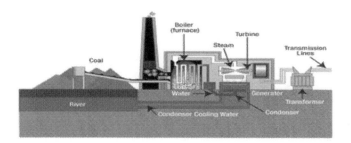

Geothermal Power Plant

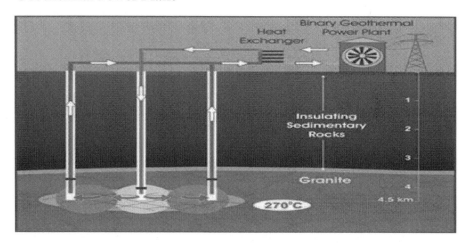

Megatech Corporation of Massachusetts manufactures geothermal laboratory equipment for students to see how thermal energy can be converted into useful power. Fortunately, the turbine engine is made of transparent materials, and the turbine operation can be seen with the naked eye. Attached to the turbine is a generator where the steam energy is converted into electrical power. The gauges will give the electrical output in amps and volts. Therefore, the power is calculated simply as:

P (power) = Amps X Volts

Earlier, it was shown that direct current (DC) can be converted into alternating current (AC) through invertors.

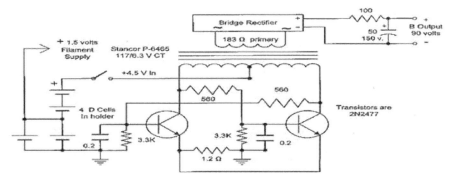

Fig. 2. Power inverter circuit operates on 4.5 volts. 1.5-volts, from two paralleled cells, is tapped off for receiver filament circuit.

Example of a power inverter circuit diagram

E. Fuel Cells

To generate power, it was shown that gas engines are the most common, followed by diesel engines. There are many moving parts in an engine, and the exhaust gases must go through a catalytic converter to reduce emissions. A power station produces electrical power with a generator; certainly, this has a lot of moving parts. Now look at a fuel cell and note that it operates more like a car battery that cranks an engine. This is why fuel cells could be one of the most attractive options for cars.

The process is shown below, and the preferred fuel is hydrogen. Hydrogen combines with oxygen and has *no* carbon emissions. The hydrogen can be combined in a fuel cell with oxygen and give useful electrical power to run an electric car. Only water, which can be recycled back to the fuel cell, is used in this process.

Fuel Cell Operation:

- It generates electrical power quietly and efficiently without pollution.

- Fuel cells take the chemical energy from different types of fuels. (Hydrogen being the best.)

- Stored chemical energy with other gaseous fuels— like natural gas—can be converted into electrical energy through a special process.

- Electrolytes act as separators and keep the reactants from mixing together.

- Electrodes are the catalysts where the electrochemical reaction occurs.

- The bi-polar plate collects the current and builds voltage from the cells.

- The anode is the negative post of the fuel cell. It conducts the electrons that are freed from the hydrogen molecules.

- The cathode is the positive post. It distributes the oxygen to the surface of the catalyst.

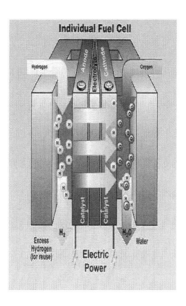

The challenging question is how to store hydrogen in a car. In its gaseous form, it must be compressed to over 10,000 psi to make it worthwhile for transport vehicles. This is a very challenging situation: both in a collision scenario and leaking H2 into a closed garage or building. There are several ways of storing H2 that could be safer (as shown below).

Hydrogen fuel can be utilized most beneficially in liquid form. This requires extremely cold storage tanks. Quite amazingly, the second stage of the Saturn Rocket engine that took astronauts to the moon used liquid hydrogen for extra boost/power.

Methods to Store Hydrogen

- Compressed Gas Storage Tanks. New tank materials (carbon fiber based) allow hydrogen to be stored at high pressure (5k to 10k psi); today, the cost is high.

- Liquid Hydrogen. Mass stored is high; the liquefaction cost is high.

- Chemical Hydrides. Pure and alloyed metals can combine with H2: cool to absorb H2 and heat to release H2; percentage stored is about 5–10 percent, by weight.

- Gas-On Solid Adsorption. Adsorb H2 on Activated Carbon; the cost is very high; the percent adsorbed is high; the percent stored is about 70 percent, by weight.

- Microspheres/Nano-Tubes. Glass spheres store H2 at high temperature & pressure; cool to store and heat to release H2. Basic R&D is progressing. Today, percent stored is about 5–10 percent, by weight.

- Molten-carbonate fuel cell (MCFC). This is best suited for large stationary power generators: just like the SOFC. This operates at high temperatures but is less expensive than the SOFC.

- Phosphoric-acid fuel cell (PAFC). This has potential for use in small stationary power-generation systems. It operates at a higher temperature than the PEMFC, so it takes longer to warm up—making it not suitable for cars.

- Direct-methanol fuel cell (DMFC). This is comparable to a PEMFC in regard to operating temperature, but is not as efficient. It uses platinum as a catalyst, which makes it much more expensive.

- Solid oxide fuel cell (SOFC). This is best suited for large-scale stationary power generators that could provide electricity for factories or towns. This type of fuel cell operates at very high temperatures. High temperatures make its reliability questionable, but it has the longest operating life.

- Alkaline fuel cell (AFC). This is one of the oldest types, and it has been used by NASA since the 1960s. It requires pure hydrogen and oxygen and is very expensive. Most likely, it can be commercialized.

12: Careers in the Energy, Power, and Transportation Industries

There are new and emerging industries, especially in the alternative energy field. America and other nations are developing more "Energy Farms" with the hope of replacing fossil fuels. Their installations require new skills that must be taught in tech schools and colleges.

The existing auto/transportation industry is expanding the technical base through specialists that are mostly ASE certified. The training programs are categorized separately from auto industry jobs that are available at all times. The purpose of this section is to offer the reader a broader outlook for career paths, rather than direct them to a specific job or to become a specialist. The following emerging industries for alternative energy jobs are as follows:

A. Hydropower
B. Solar PV
C. Wind
D. Geothermal
E. Fuel cell
F. Automotive
   1. Electric
   2. Hybrids
   3. Advanced direct fuel injection
   4. Alternative fuel engines
   5. Biodiesel fuels

The job opportunities vary by state, since each state develops its own energy resources. For example, the West and Southwest have plenty of sunny days that make solar energy flourish. Wind farms are localized in certain regions of the United States, and geothermal follows the same. The following chart shows relatively the number of people employed in the alternative energy industry.

Where are the Jobs?

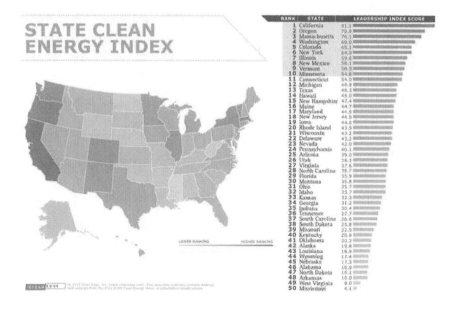

STATE CLEAN ENERGY INDEX

RANK	STATE	LEADERSHIP INDEX SCORE
1	California	93.1
2	Oregon	79.9
3	Massachusetts	76.1
4	Washington	69.0
5	Colorado	65.1
6	New York	64.9
7	Illinois	59.6
8	New Mexico	58.1
9	Vermont	56.5
10	Minnesota	54.8
11	Connecticut	54.0
12	Michigan	48.9
13	Texas	48.3
14	Hawaii	48.0
15	New Hampshire	47.4
16	Maine	44.7
17	Maryland	44.6
18	New Jersey	44.6
19	Iowa	44.6
20	Rhode Island	43.5
21	Wisconsin	43.2
22	Delaware	43.2
23	Nevada	42.0
24	Pennsylvania	40.1
25	Arizona	39.0
26	Utah	38.1
27	Virginia	37.6
28	North Carolina	36.7
29	Florida	35.9
30	Montana	35.8
31	Ohio	35.7
32	Idaho	35.7
33	Kansas	32.3
34	Georgia	31.2
35	Indiana	30.4
36	Tennessee	27.3
37	South Carolina	26.6
38	South Dakota	25.8
39	Missouri	22.5
40	Kentucky	20.8
41	Oklahoma	20.2
42	Alaska	19.8
43	Louisiana	18.9
44	Wyoming	17.4
45	Nebraska	17.3
46	Alabama	16.9
47	North Dakota	16.1
48	Arkansas	16.0
49	West Virginia	8.0
50	Mississippi	4.3

LOWER RANKING   HIGHER RANKING

At this stage, it is more appropriate to merge the job descriptions rather than define the differences.

1. **Hydropower Plant Engineer**

   These jobs are defined in terms of: site evaluation, sizing power plant generator, preparing preliminary proposals, economics, and environmental issues. They act as consultants and senior engineers.

2. **Sales Engineers**

   These positions are very common with micro-hydropower installations projects. The sales engineer prepares preliminary proposals that show the potential benefits of the project, basic specifications, cost, and benefit. The educational background is mostly in electrical engineering with a BS degree or a mechanical engineer with a BS degree.

3. **Installation Tech**

   This type of work is very broad, depending on the size of the plant. It will require knowledge and skills in: construction, plumbing, electrical, and many other trades that technical schools/colleges provide.

4. **Operations Manager**

   This position is usually assigned to a person who has "gone through" a construction phase of a plant or a well-trained electrical engineer with many years of experience. He or she is responsible for: overlooking the entire operation (including power efficiency requirements), manpower, monitoring the plant's instrumentation, and maintenance needs. For small micro-sized plants, this position can be filled by a well-rounded electrical engineer with a BS degree or better.

5. **Hydro-Plant Maintenance Tech**

   All power plants employ one or more maintenance techs with backgrounds in a few trade areas: such as plumbing, electrical, wiring, and welding/construction. The training is available through community colleges where an Associate's degree is obtained upon completion of a two-year program.

6. **Environmental Engineer**

   This requires someone who has studied at a college or university and obtained a BS degree or better. They prepare all the preliminary reports, permits and cite conditions and assess environmental impact.

An important website by O.NET Online (please refer to their site: onetonline.org) conducted an industry-wide search for job titles and tasks expected from a person with the title of:

Hydroelectric Plant Technician

Tasks:

- Identify or address malfunctions of hydroelectric plant operational equipment, such as generators, transformers, or turbines.

- Monitor hydroelectric power plant equipment operation and performance, adjusting to performance specifications, as necessary.

- Start, adjust, or stop generating units, operating valves, gates, or auxiliary equipment, in hydroelectric power generating plants.

- Communicate status of hydroelectric operating equipment to despatchers or supervisors.

- Implement load or switching orders in hydroelectric plants, in accordance with specifications or instructions.

- Inspect water-powered electric generators or auxiliary equipment in hydroelectric plants to verify proper operations or to determine maintenance or repair needs.

- Install or calibrate electric or mechanical equipment, such as: motors, engines, switchboards, relays, switch gears, meters, pumps, hydraulics, or flood channels.

- Maintain logs, reports, work requests, or other records of work performed in hydroelectric plants.

- Maintain or repair hydroelectric plant electrical, mechanical, or electronic equipment, such as: motors, transformers, voltage regulators, generators, relays, battery systems, air compressors, sump pumps, gates, or valves.

- Operate high voltage switches or related device in hydropower stations.

Hydroelectric Production Manager

Tasks:

- Direct operations, maintenance, or repair of hydroelectric power facilities.

- Supervise or monitor hydroelectric facility operations to ensure that generation or mechanical equipment conform to applicable regulations or standards.

- Check hydroelectric operations for compliance with prescribed operating limits, such as: loads, voltages, temperatures, lines, or equipment.

- Create or enforce hydro station voltage schedules.

- Develop or review: budgets, annual plans, power contracts, power rates, standing operating procedures, power reviews, or engineering studies.

- Identify and communicate power system emergencies.

- Inspect hydroelectric facilities, including switchyards, control houses, or relay houses, for normal operation or adherence to safety standards.

- Maintain records of hydroelectric facility operations, maintenance, or repairs.

- Monitor or inspect hydroelectric equipment, such as: hydro-turbines, generators, or control systems.

- Negotiate power generation contracts with other public or private utilities.

Certainly, this section gives the reader an idea on what kind of work is involved with various positions.

Besides the total number of jobs, it is just as important to pick a trade/engineering school that meets the demand of the industries. The job descriptions are intended as a guide; the emerging industries are clarifying and assigning the task as the number of employees grows in each particular sector.

Hydropower.

This industry has been well-established and has been around for centuries. The Hoover Dam was constructed in 1938. During construction, the project employed thousands of workers. Now, it is scaled down to focus on maintenance and some engineering to improve the efficiency of the total system. These types of power plants produce well over one thousand megawatts and up.

a. Micro-hydropower plants:

They differ in use and applications toward smaller, remote towns or industries. They are on the other extreme of the Hoover Dam. The power output can vary from one Kilowatt to several megawatts of power. This industry is continuing to grow due to its quicker applications compared to extensive studies needed for the mega-sized dams.

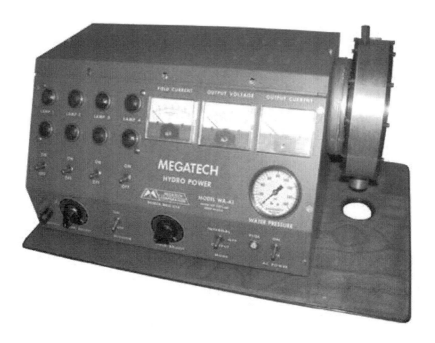

Megatech model MEGWA: Hydropower Trainer

Solar Careers:

The solar energy industry is divided into two specializations:
- photovoltaic (PV) panel manufacturers and installers, and
- solar thermal panel manufacturers and installers.

The first one is designed to generate electrical power and has received the largest support from power companies. Large installations can produce millions of watts, which can be connected to the power grid. This process helps the power companies, because they can sell it to the consumer and avoid building more power plants, which requires huge capital investments. In the West and Southwest, there are PV installations generating power in the hundreds of megawatts range. During construction, they employ technicians and construction workers by the hundreds.

The solar thermal panel manufacturers are mostly focused on residential domestic hot water needs. Homes, on the average, consume 30 percent of their energy in hot water for domestic use (i.e., showers, laundry, dishwashers, etc.). Pool heating is another area where solar thermal panels can save the consumer considerable amounts of money. This is why small businesses, various schools, and hospitals have installed solar thermal panels.

The solar energy industry has emerged in two different directions. The ones that design, produce, and install PV panels usually have education in electrical engineering. Those who install have technical knowledge and are graduates from community colleges and technical schools. Solar thermal systems training programs are offered in community colleges and trade schools.

Career Path for Solar Energy Industry

Photovoltaic Systems

1. **Systems Designer:** Sizes, estimates, and prepares proposals

2. **R&D Engineer:** Develops higher efficiency PV panels

3. **Solar PV Technician:** Installs PV panels

4. **Solar PV Production Tech:** Manufactures PV panels

5. **Solar Operations Manager:** Oversees installation and production

6. **Solar Maintenance Tech** Checks the electrical and mechanical parts of the installation

Solar Thermal Systems

1. **Systems Designer:** Decides the number of panels needed for a given location

2. **Sales Person/Tech:** Prepares cost figures for end users

3. **Installer:** Properly installs the panels, piping, valves and controls

4. **Assembler:** Works in factories that manufacture thermal panels

5. **Solar Pool-Heater Tech:** Sizes panels to heat pools and meet home heating needs

The website of O*Net Online, onetonline.org, has done preliminary searches into the solar industry and has displayed the following positions and task lists, as seen below:

Solar Energy Systems Engineers
Perform site-specific engineering analysis or evaluation of energy efficiency and solar projects involving residential, commercial, or industrial customers. Design solar domestic hot water and space heating systems for new and existing structures, applying knowledge of structural energy requirements, local climates, solar technology, and thermodynamics.

Tasks:

- Conduct engineering site audits to collect structural, electrical, and related site information for use in the design of residential or commercial solar power systems.

- Design or coordinate design of photovoltaic (PV) or solar thermal systems, including system components, for residential and commercial buildings.

- Create checklists for review or inspection of completed solar installations projects.

- Create electrical single-line diagrams, panel schedules, or connection diagrams for solar electric systems using computer-aided design (CAD) software.

- Create plans for solar energy system development, monitoring, and evaluation activities.

- Develop design specifications and functional requirements for residential, commercial, or industrial solar energy systems or components.

- Perform computer simulation of solar photovoltaic (PV) generation system performance or energy production to optimize efficiency.

- Provide technical direction or support to installation teams during installation, start-up, testing, system commissioning, or performance monitoring.

- Design or develop vacuum tube collector systems for solar applications.

- Develop standard operating procedures and quality or safety standards for solar installation work.

Energy Engineers

Design, develop, or evaluate energy-related projects or programs to reduce energy costs or improve energy efficiency during the designing, building, or remodeling stages of construction. May specialize in electrical systems; heating, ventilation, and air-condition (HVAC) systems; green buildings; lighting; air quality; or energy procurement.

Sample of reported job titles:

Energy Efficiency Engineer, Energy Manager, Distributed Generation Project Manager, Energy Engineer, Environmental Solutions Engineer, Industrial Energy Engineer, Measurement and Verification Engineer, Test and Balance Engineer

Tasks:

- Identify energy savings opportunities and make recommendations to achieve more energy-efficient operation.

- Manage the development, design or construction of energy conservation projects to ensure acceptability of budgets and time lines, conformance to federal and state laws, or adherence to approved specifications.

- Conduct energy audits to evaluate energy use, costs, or conservation measures.

- Monitor and analyze energy consumption.

- Perform: energy modeling, measurement, verification, commissioning, or retro-commissioning.

- Oversee design or construction aspects related to energy, such as: energy engineering, energy management, and sustainable design.

- Conduct jobsite observations, field inspections, and sub-metering to collect data for energy conservation analyses.

- Review architectural, mechanical, or electrical plans and specifications to evaluate energy efficiency or determine economic, service, or engineering feasibility.

- Inspect or monitor energy systems, including heating, ventilating, and air conditioning (HVAC) or day lighting systems to determine energy use or potential energy savings.

- Evaluate construction design information, such as: detail and assembly drawings, design calculations, system layouts and sketches, or specifications.

Solar Sales

Contact customer to determine his or her solar equipment needs, suggest systems or equipment, list and prepare an estimate.

Tasks:

- Prepare proposals, quotes, contracts, or presentations for potential solar customers.

- Select solar energy products, systems, or services for customers based on: electrical energy requirements, site conditions, price, or other factors.

- Provide customers with information, such as: quotes, orders, sales, shipping, warranties, credit, funding options, incentives, or tax rebates.

- Gather information from prospective customers to identify their solar energy needs.

- Provide technical information about solar power, solar systems, equipment, and services to potential customers or dealers.

- Calculate potential solar resources or solar array production for a particular site, considering issues such as climate, shading, and roof orientation.

- Generate solar energy customer leads to develop new accounts.

- Take quote requests or orders from dealers or customers.

- Assess sites to determine suitability for solar equipment, using equipment such as: tape measures, compasses, and computer software.

- Prepare or review detailed design drawings, specifications, or lists related to solar installations.

Solar Energy Installation Managers

Direct work crews installing residential or commercial solar photovoltaic or thermal systems.

Tasks:

- Plan and coordinate installations of photovoltaic (PV) solar and solar thermal systems to ensure conformance to codes.

- Supervise solar installers, technicians, and subcontractors for solar installation projects to ensure compliance with safety standards.

- Assess potential solar installation sites to determine feasibility and design requirements.

- Assess system performance or functionality at the system, subsystem, and component levels.

- Coordinate or schedule building inspections for solar installation projects.

- Monitor work of contractors and subcontractors to ensure projects conform to: plans, specifications, schedules, or budgets.

- Perform start-up of systems for testing or customer implementation.

- Provide technical assistance to installers, technicians, or other solar professionals in areas such as: solar electric systems, solar thermal systems, electrical systems, and mechanical systems.

- Visit customer sites to determine solar system needs, requirements, or specifications.

- Develop and maintain system architecture, including all piping, instrumentation, or process-flow diagrams.

Solar Thermal Installers and Technicians

Install or repair solar energy systems designed to collect, store, and circulate solar-heated water for residential, commercial, or industrial use.

Tasks:

- Design active direct or indirect, passive direct or indirect, or pool solar systems.

- Perform routine maintenance or repairs to restore solar thermal systems to baseline operating conditions.

- Apply operation or identification tags or labels to system components, as required.

- Assess collector sites to ensure structural integrity of potential mounting surfaces or the best orientation and tilt for solar collectors.

- Connect water heaters and storage tanks to power and water sources.

- Determine locations for installing solar subsystem components, including: piping, water heaters, valves, and ancillary equipment.

- Fill water tanks and check tanks pipes and fitting for leaks.

- Identify plumbing, electrical, environmental, or safety hazards associated with solar thermal installations.

- Install circulating pumps using: pipe, fittings, soldering equipment, electrical supplies, and hand tools.

- Install copper or plastic plumbing, using: pipes, fittings, pipe cutters, acetylene torches, solder, wire brushes, sand cloths, flux, plastic pipe cleaners, or plastic glue.

Solar Photovoltaic Installers

Assemble, install, or maintain solar photovoltaic (PV) systems on roofs or other structures in compliance with site assessment and schematics. May include: measuring, cutting, assembling, and bolting structural framing and solar modules. May perform minor electrical work such as current checks.

Tasks:

- Install photovoltaic (PV) systems in accordance with codes and standards using drawings, schematics, and instructions.

- Assemble solar modules, panels, or support structures, as specified.

- Apply weather sealing to array, building, or support mechanisms.

- Determine appropriate sizes, ratings, and locations for all system: overcurrent devices disconnect devices, grounding equipment, and surge suppressions equipment.

- Install module array interconnect wiring, implementing measures to disable arrays during installation.

- Identify methods for lying out, orienting, and mounting modules or arrays to ensure efficient installation, electrical configuration, or system maintenance.

- Identify electrical, environmental, and safety hazards associated with photovoltaic (PV) installations.

- Examine designs to determine current requirements for all parts of the photovoltaic (PV) system electrical circuit.

- Check electrical installation for: proper wiring, polarity, grounding, or integrity or terminations.

- Test operating voltages to ensure operation with acceptable limits for power conditioning equipment, such as: inverters and controllers.

Wind Turbines and Careers

"Wind farm" is a term used to name a large power production facility that uses tens and hundreds of wind turbines in a large field. Recently, some sites are producing over two thousand megawatts of power. That is the equivalent of two *nuclear* power plants. Wind is a renewable energy source, and there are many locations in the United States that use it. In terms of careers, large facilities require considerable environmental studies compared to small, one-unit locations at a home or farm. Most jobs currently are in the fabrications of the wind turbines for large facilities. The job categories and skills vary based on the number of wind turbines to be installed on an approved land.

1. **Wind Energy Analyst**
   Takes measurement of the average wind velocity over the land, history, and seasonal variations and provides the data to the systems engineer.

2. **Wind Turbine Engineers**
   They are design engineers who size wind turbines to match the available energy in the wind.

3. **Wind Systems Project Engineer**

   Oversees the project engineering, provides the power output information to the utility companies, and assures that all technical design and data are reliable.

4. **Wind Turbine Tech**

   The technical installation is done by specially trained technicians who are familiar in building towers that can stand up to storms, heat, cold, and other conditions.

5. **Wind Turbine Assembler**

   This position requires assembly training inside the factory. They make the blades of the turbine, assemble the gear box, and do electrical wiring and controls.

6. **Wind Farm Maintenance Tech**

   Once the system is in operation, it requires troubleshooting for any electrical/mechanical failure that happens to the installation.

7. Wind Turbine Operations Manager

This person assures that when the demand is high for electricity by the power company, all systems are ready for the demand. Certainly, there is no guarantee that the wind is available on the exact days or weeks when wind energy is most needed. The utilities would like to store wind energy if storage can be done in a cost-effective manner. For small one-unit sites, it is easily stored in batteries.

Onetonline.org has conducted preliminary research for the wind turbine service technicians and lists the tasks as follows:

Wind Turbine Service Technicians

Inspect, diagnose, adjust, or repair wind turbines. Perform maintenance on wind turbine equipment, including: resolving electrical, mechanical, and hydraulic malfunctions.

Tasks:

- Inspect or repair fiberglass turbine blades.

- Troubleshoot or repair mechanical, hydraulic, or electrical malfunctions related to: variable pitch systems, variable speed control systems, converter systems, or related components.

- Climb wind turbine towers to inspect, maintain, or repair equipment.

- Diagnose problems involving wind turbine generators or control systems.

- Perform routine maintenance on: wind turbine equipment, underground transmission systems, wind fields substations, or fiber-optic sensing and control systems.

- Start or restart wind turbine generator systems to ensure proper operations.

- Test electrical components of wind systems with devices, such as: voltage testers, multimeters, oscilloscopes, infrared testers, or fiber-optic equipment.

- Test structures, controls, or mechanical, hydraulic, or electrical systems, according to test plans or in coordination with engineers.

- Assist in assembly of individual wind generators or construction of wind farms.

- Collect turbine data for testing or research and analysis.

Wind Energy Project Managers

Lead or manage the development and evaluation of potential wind energy business opportunities, including: environmental studies, permitting, and proposals. May also manage construction of projects.

Tasks:

- Create wind energy project plans, including: project scope, goals, tasks, resources, schedules, costs, contingencies, or other project information.

- Prepare or assist in the preparation of applications for environmental, building, or other required permits.

- Coordinate or direct development, energy assessment, engineering, or construction activities to ensure that wind project needs and objectives are met.

- Develop scope of work for wind project functions, such as: design, site assessment, environmental studies, surveying, or field support services.

- Manage wind project costs to stay within budget limits.

- Prepare wind project documentation, including: diagrams or layouts.

- Provide technical support for design, construction, or commissioning of wind farm projects.

- Provide verbal or written project status reports to: project teams, management, subcontractors, customers, or owners.

- Review civil design, engineering, or construction technical documentation to ensure compliance with applicable government or industrial codes, standards, requirements, or regulations.

- Review or evaluate proposals or bids to make recommendations regarding awarding of contracts.

Wind Energy Operations Managers

Manage wind field operations, including: personnel, maintenance activities, financial activities, and planning.

Tasks:

- Oversee the maintenance of wind field equipment or structures, such as: towers, transformers, electrical collector systems, roadways, or other site assets.

- Prepare wind field operational budgets.

- Supervise employees or subcontractors to ensure quality of work or adherence to safety regulations or policies.

- Develop processes or procedures for wind operations, including transitioning from construction to commercial operations.

- Develop relationships and communicate with: customers, site managers, developers, land owners, authorities, utility representatives, or residents.

- Establish goals, objectives, or priorities for wind field operations.

- Estimate costs associated with operations, including repairs or preventive maintenance.

- Monitor and maintain records of daily facility operations.

- Review, negotiate, or approve wind farm contracts.

- Recruit or select wind operations employees, contractors, or subcontractors.

Wind Energy Engineers
Design underground or overhead wind farm collector systems and prepare and develop site specifications.

Tasks:

- Create or maintain wind farm layouts, schematics, or other visual documentations for wind farms.

- Recommend process or infrastructure changes to improve wind turbine performances, reduce operational costs, or comply with regulations.

- Create models to optimize the layout of wind farm's: access roads, crane pads, crane paths, collections systems, substations, switchyards, or transmissions lines.

- Provide engineering technical support to designers of prototype wind turbines.

- Investigate experimental wind turbines or wind turbine technologies for properties, such as: aerodynamics, production, noise, and load.

- Develop active control algorithms, electronics, software, electromechanical, or electrohydraulic systems for wind turbines.

- Develop specifications for wind technology components, such as: gearboxes, blades, generators, frequency converters, and pad transformers.

- Test wind turbine components, using mechanical or electronic testing equipment.

- Oversee the work activities of wind farm consultants or subcontractors.

- Test wind turbine equipment to determine effects of stress or fatigue.

Geothermal Power Plant Careers

Utility companies have partnered with private corporations to build power plants that use the earth's geothermal energy. This source could develop into a multi-megawatt power that could match the power output of a nuclear power station. After all, the earth's core acts like a nuclear reactor, and engineers have designed ways to tap into it.

The careers and jobs are site-dependent. In the United States, there are certain locations that geothermal energy is available without drilling thousands of feet into the earth's crust. The following represents some of the career paths available.

1. **Geologists**
   They have the skills to do a site evaluation and prepare reports on the environment where the power plant will be located.

2. **Power Plant Systems Engineer**
   Since the earth's energy is converted to steam, the turbine generators are similar to a coal-fired power plant. This person

evaluates all engineering instrumentation on the supply side of the geothermal wells and properly sizes the turbine generators.

3. **Geothermal Power Plant Tech:**
   These technicians are skilled in piping, welding and installing steam/hot water pipes from the source of heat to the condensers where the steam gives off the heat.

4. **Operations Engineer**
   The proper power output and the connecting to the power grid depend on the operations engineer. This is one of the high-paying positions, because the profitability depends on how efficiently the system is operating.

5. **Maintenance Engineer**
   The energy source—being deep wells—could change due to unknown shifts in temperature. The output power could vary, and the maintenance engineer must keep track of all readings in the control room. Any problems are brought to the attention of the chief engineer/systems engineer for evaluation.

Once again, onetonline.org has listed the job and task list as follows:

Geothermal Technicians

Perform technical activities at power plants or individual installations necessary for the generation of power from geothermal energy sources. Monitor and control operating activities at geothermal power generation facilities and perform maintenance and repairs as necessary. Install, test, and maintain residential and commercial geothermal heat pumps.

Tasks:

- Identify and correct malfunctions of geothermal plant equipment, electrical systems, instrumentation or controls

- Monitor and adjust operations of geothermal power plant equipment or systems.

- Adjust power production systems to meet load and distribution demands.

- Collect and record data associated with operating geothermal power plants or well fields.

- Prepare and maintain logs, reports, or other documentation of work performed.

- Install and maintain geothermal plant electrical protection equipment.

- Maintain electrical switchgear, process controls, transmitters, gauges, and control equipment in accordance with geothermal plant procedures.

- Maintain, calibrate, or repair plant instrumentation, control, and electronic devices in geothermal plants.

- Determine whether emergency or auxiliary systems will be needed to keep properties heated or cold in extreme weather conditions.

- Test water sources for factors, such as: flow volume and contaminant presence.

Geothermal Production Managers

Manage operations at geothermal power generation facilities. Maintain and monitor geothermal plant equipment for efficient and safe plant operations.

Tasks:

- Supervise employees in geothermal power plants or well fields. Oversee geothermal plant operations, maintenance, and repairs to ensure compliance with applicable standards or regulations.

- Communicate geothermal plant conditions to employees.

- Identify and evaluate equipment, procedural, or conditional inefficiencies involving geothermal plant systems.

- Perform or direct the performance of preventative maintenance on geothermal plant equipment.

- Inspect geothermal plant or injection well fields to verify proper equipment operations.

- Develop or manage budgets for geothermal operations.

- Select and implement corrosion control or mitigation systems for geothermal plants.
- Develop operating plans and schedules for geothermal operations.
- Record, review or maintain daily logs, reports, maintenance, and other records associated with geothermal operations.

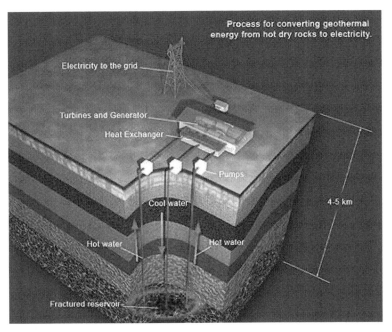

Fuel Cell Careers

Even though fuel cells have been around for a long time, they represent many challenges to be utilized with passenger cars. This technology was used on the Apollo capsules to provide power for the astronauts that landed on the moon. Yet, these systems are not in cars but on the ground being used as power plants for certain industries and businesses. Regardless, this field is quite exciting because of its potential to replace reciprocating engines. This industry will grow if the cost is brought down to reasonable levels that can compare with gas and diesel generators.

1. **Electrical/Chemical R&D Engineer**
   The federal government and auto industry have combined their resources to research new materials and chemicals that can generate electricity at a higher efficiency.

2. **R&D Technician**
   Prototypes are constantly being built and improved by engineers and technicians who do the physical work rather than the theoretical work.

3. **Electric Vehicle Tech**
   Fuel cells are installed in electric cars that are modified by these techs. At times, they are capable of removing gas engines and converting them to electric vehicles. Once the designs are approved, the auto industry will open its doors to many manufacturing jobs. Currently, there are jobs for ground installations that generate power in the several-thousand-watt range outputs and up to megawatt range. The installers have similar backgrounds to solar PV installers.

A worker prepares a nickel plate for a fuel cell inside the Fuel Cell Energy manufacturing facility in Torrington, Connecticut.

13: ASE/NATEF Standards

Gas Powered Engine

Hybrid Car

Truck

The auto industry is one of the largest employers in the United States and needed to establish an organized approach to encourage students to be employed in its fields. As such, they helped to create a non-profit organization, NATEF, the abbreviation for "National Automotive Technicians Education Foundation," which publishes the task lists to be taught by schools. With this standard, the auto industry in all fifty states can have a person that has met the "standards" and is ASE certified without any doubts about his or her education and automotive background. The NATEF organization was founded in 1983 for the sole purpose that is quoted on their website: "to evaluate technician training programs against standards developed by the automotive industry and recommend qualifying programs for NATEF accreditation."

As this brief paragraph states, the training and career path becomes closer in the minds of students/adults who want to be employed in the auto industry.

The headquarters of NATEF:
101 Blue Seal Drive, Suite 101
Leesburg, VA 20175
Telephone: (703) 669-6650

In the next section, the importance of science, technology, engineering and math (S.T.E.M.) will be shown as vital in an advancing automotive technician. The engineering for new hybrids, electric vehicles, and alternatively fueled vehicles all point towards the need for S.T.E.M. In addition, the proper use of technical terms, definitions, and communication become the foundation of an ever-learning technician. These guidelines are developed and available on the NATEF website and are best described by their own write-up:

The intent of this document is twofold: (1) to serve as a resource to educational institutions and automotive technology teachers in planning, preparing, delivering, and assessing instructional content for preparing automotive technicians of the future; and (2) to demonstrate the extent to which today's automotive technician is dependent upon and must be competent in the application of appropriate math, science, and communications skills in the day-to-day performance of his or her job.

The above phrase must be translated into effective learning and practices through specialized labs that tie in sciences and languages to hands-on skills.

Megatech Corporation has manufactured (and is the only manufacturer) of an oil-less, transparent engine which operates with any gaseous/liquid fuel. It is part of the alternative fuel training. As of today, this engine is found in all fifty states and over thirty nations.

Automobile Minimum Requirements

1. The minimum program requirements are identical for initial accreditation and for renewal of accreditation.

2. Programs must meet the following hour requirements based on the level of accreditation sought.

Maintenance & Light Repair

-   **540 hours** combined classroom and lab/shop instructional activities

Automobile Service Technology

-   **840 hours** combined classroom and lab/shop instructional activities

Master Automobile Service Technology

-   **1080 hours** combined classroom and lab/shop instructional activities

3. **The average rating on each of Standards 6, 7, 8, and 9 found on the NATEF website must be a four** on the five-point scale. The program will not be approved for an on-site evaluation if the average is less than four on any of those standards. The program should make improvements before submitting the application to NATEF for review. **A program will be denied accreditation if the on-site evaluation team average on Standards 6, 7, 8, or 9 is less than four.**

4. A "Yes" response must be achieved on all six criteria in Standard 11 if the program is using it to meet the instructional hour requirements for the purpose of accreditation. The program will not be approved for an on-site evaluation if it cannot support a "Yes" response to each criterion on the self-evaluation. *A program will be denied accreditation if the*

on-site evaluation team does not give a "Yes" response to all six criteria in Standard 11. This applies only to programs using the provisions in Standard 11 for the purpose of meeting instructional hour requirements.

5. A program may not be approved for an on-site evaluation if the average rating on Standards 1–5 and 10 is less than a four on the five-point scale. **A program may be denied accreditation if the on-site evaluation team average on Standards 1–5 and 10 is less than four.** Approval for on-site evaluation or accreditation will be made by NATEF, based on the number of standards rated at four or five as well as the individual rating on any standard rated less than four.

6. All MLR instructors must be ASE certified in A4, A5, A6, and A8. All AST and MAST instructors must hold current ASE certification in A6 and in the automobile area(s) (A1, A2, A3, A4, A5, A7, and A8) they teach.

7. All instructors must attend a minimum of twenty hours per year of recognized industry update training relevant to their program.

8. The program Advisory Committee must conduct at least two working meetings a year and must have a minimum of five people (excluding school personnel) on the committee. Minutes of the meetings must be provided to the on-site evaluation team for review and must reflect relevant areas of the standards as having been considered by the Advisory Committee.

9. The NATEF Standards recognize that program content requirements vary by program type and by regional employment needs. Therefore, flexibility has been built into the

NATEF task list by assigning each task a priority number. A program must include in their curriculum the designated percentage of tasks in each priority numbered category (P-1, P-2, and P-3) in order to be accredited. The following percentages are required:

95% of all Priority 1 (P-1) tasks must be taught.
80% of all Priority 2 (P-2) tasks must be taught.
50% of all Priority 3 (P-3) tasks must be taught.

10. The concern for safety is paramount to the learning environment. Each program level has the following safety requirement preceding all related tasks:

Comply with personal and environmental safety practices associated with clothing; eye protection; hand tools; power equipment; proper ventilation; and the handling, storage, and disposal of chemicals/materials in accordance with local, state, and federal safety and environmental regulations.

The information above can be found on
www.natef.org in more detail.

14: Jobs and Careers in the Auto/Trucking Industries

The auto industry is well-structured in terms of dealerships, manufacturing jobs, sales, and service. To implement an effective training program, they have assisted schools in establishing standards that are set by ASE/NATEF. The NATEF website offers the entire list of tasks that an automotive student should be able to do to achieve certain specializations, as follows:

1. Engine repair

2. Automotive transmission and transaxle repair

3. Manual drivetrain and axles

4. Suspension and steering

5. Brakes

6. Electrical/electronic systems

7. Heating, ventilation, and air conditioning

8. Engine performance

In order to be qualified to get jobs, training programs are available starting in high schools and advancing into colleges. After a choice is made in one or more of the above specifications, a test is offered by ASE/NATEF in order to be qualified and hired by dealerships. The auto industry is very large and offers many jobs in ever-changing car designs. Electric cars, hybrids, diesels, and many sizes/models compound the choices. It is best to identify which areas interest the individual, and then receive the certification in that area.

The Department of Labor publishes in various categories the number of service techs and dealership employment numbers by state and wages. The following is a brief summary to help a person realize how large the choices are in various services. The person could be in one or more of these sectors of the transportation industry:

A. Automotive Technician

B. Autobody Technician

C. Truck Technician

D. Parts Specialist

E. Alternative Fuel Vehicle (AFV) Technician

Any Technician that can master all eight areas of the specializations and is ASE certified can earn over $60,000 a year.

The following statistics are offered on the ASE's official website, ase. com, and are included here to offer the reader an idea on how diverse and numerous the career opportunities are in the automotive industry.

Master Automobile Technicians	93,341
Master Collision Repair/Refinish Technicians	5,722
Master Medium/Heavy Truck Technicians	14,532
Master Medium/Heavy Vehicle Technicians	227
Master Truck Equipment Technicians	1,399
Master Engine Machinists	1,338
Master Transit Bus Technicians	576
Master School Bus Technicians	1,873

Automobile Series	
A1: Engine Repair	163,376
A2: Automatic Transmission Transaxle	114,337
A3: Manual Drive Train and Axles	129,223
A4: Suspension and Steering	189,424
A5: Brakes	208,480
A6: Electrical/Electronic Systems	166,406
A7: Heating and Air Conditioning	153,037
A8: Engine Performance	150,809
A9: Light Vehicle Diesel Engines	10,019

Automotive Service Technicians and Mechanics

Considerable information is available through the Bureau of Labor Statistics, US Department of Labor's occupational outlook handbook: 2012-13 edition, wages and employment trends nationally.

National:
Median wages (2011) $17.39 hourly, 36,180
Employment (2010) 723,000 employees
Projected growth (2010-2020) Average (10–19%)
Projected job openings: 311,700

Automotive Engineers
Develop new or improved designs for vehicle structural members, engines, transmissions, or other vehicle systems, using computer-assisted design technology. Direct building, modification, or testing of vehicle or components.

Tasks:

- Conduct or direct system-level automotive testing.

- Design control systems or algorithms for purposes, such: as automotive energy management, emissions management, or increased operational safety, or performance.

- Design or analyze automobile systems in areas, such as: aerodynamics, alternate fuels, ergonomics, hybrid power, brakes, transmissions, steering, calibration, safety, or diagnostics.

- Alter or modify designs to obtain specified functional or operational performance.

- Build models for algorithm or control feature verification testing.

- Calibrate vehicle systems, including control algorithms or other software systems.

- Conduct automotive design reviews.

- Develop calibration methodologies, test methodologies, or tools.

- Develop engineering specifications or cost estimates for automotive design concepts.

- Develop or integrate control feature requirements.

Wages & Employment Trends

National:

Median wages (2011): $38.09 hourly, $79,230 annual

Employment (2010): 243,000 employees

Projected growth (2010-2020): Slower than average (3– 9%)

Projected Job Openings (2010-2020): 99,600

Top Industries (2010): Manufacturing, professional, scientific, and technical services

Automotive Body and Related Repairers
Repair and refinish automotive vehicle bodies and straighten vehicle frames.

Tasks:

- Follow supervisors' instructions as to which parts to restore or replace and how much time the job should take.

- Review damage reports, prepare or review repair cost estimates, and plan work to be performed.

- Sand body areas to be painted and cover bumpers, windows, and trim with masking tape or paper to protect them from the paint.

- Fit and weld replacement parts into place, using wrenches and welding equipment, and grind down welds to smooth them, using power grinders and other tools.

- Prime and paint repaired surfaces, using paint spray guns and motorized sanders.

- Remove damaged sections of vehicles, using metal-cutting guns, air grinders and wrenches, and install replacement parts using wrenches or welding equipment.

- Chain or clamp frames and sections to alignment machines that use hydraulic pressure to align damaged components.

- Fill small dents that cannot be worked out with plastic or solder.

- File, grind, sand, and smooth filled or repaired surfaces, using power tools and hand tools.

- Remove upholstery, accessories, electrical window-and-seat-operating equipment, and trim to gain access to vehicle bodies and fenders.

Automotive Specialty Technicians

Repair only one system or component on a vehicle, such as: brakes, suspension, or radiator.

Tasks:

- Examine vehicles, compile estimates of repair costs, and secure customers' approval to perform repairs.

- Repair, overhaul, or adjust automobile brake systems.

- Troubleshoot fuel, ignition, and emissions control systems, using electronic testing equipment.

- Repair or replace defective ball joint suspensions, brake shoes, or wheel bearings.

- Inspect and test new vehicles for damage and record findings so that necessary repairs can be made.

- Test electronic computer components in automobiles to ensure proper operation.

- Tune automobile engines to ensure proper and efficient functioning.

- Install or repair air conditioners and service components, such as: compressors, condensers, and controls.

- Repair, replace, or adjust defective fuel injectors, carburetor parts, and gasoline filters.

- Remove and replace defective mufflers and tailpipes.

Automotive and Watercraft Service Attendants

Service automobiles, buses, trucks, boats, and other automotive or marine vehicles with fuel, lubricants, and accessories. Collect payment for services and supplies. May lubricate vehicle, change motor oil, install antifreeze, or replace lights or other accessories, such as: windshield wiper blades or fan belts. May repair or replace tires.

Tasks:

- Collect cash payments from customers and make change or charge purchases to customers' credit cards and provide customers with receipts.

- Activate fuel pumps and fill fuel tanks of vehicles with gasoline or diesel fuel to specified levels.

- Prepare daily reports of fuel, oil, and accessory sales.

- Clean parking areas, offices, restrooms, or equipment and remove trash.

- Check air pressure in vehicle tires; check levels of fuel, motor oil, transmission, radiator, battery, and other fluids; and add air, oil, water, or other fluids, as required.

- Clean windshields, and/or wash and wax vehicles.

- Provide customers with information about local roads or highways.

- Perform minor repairs, such as: adjusting brakes, replacing spark plugs, or changing engine oil or filters.

- Order stock and price and shelve incoming goods.

- Rotate, test, and repair or replace tires.

Truck Diesel Engine Mechanics and Specialists

The trucking industry depends heavily on diesel engines to power trucks and buses. The following statistics offer the reader an idea how many people work in servicing trucks and buses.

Bus and Truck Mechanics and Diesel Engine Specialists
Diagnose, adjust, repair, or overhaul buses and trucks, or maintain and repair any type of diesel engines. Includes mechanics working primarily with automobile or marine diesel engines.

Tasks:

- Use hand tools, such as: screwdrivers, pliers, wrenches, pressure gauges, and precision instruments, as well as power tools, such: as pneumatic wrenches, lathes, welding equipment, and jacks and hoists.

- Inspect brake systems, steering mechanisms, wheel bearings, and other important parts to ensure that they are in proper operating condition.

- Adjust and reline brakes, align wheels, tighten bolts and screws, and reassemble equipment.

- Raise trucks, buses, and heavy parts or equipment, using hydraulic jacks or hoists.

- Perform routine maintenance, such as: changing oil, checking batteries, and lubricating equipment and machinery.

- Test drive trucks and buses to diagnose malfunctions or to ensure that they are working properly.

- Examine and adjust protective guards, loose bolts, and specified safety devices.

- Attach test instruments to equipment and read dials and gauges to diagnose malfunctions.

- Inspect, test, and listen to defective equipment to diagnose malfunctions, using test instruments, such as: handheld computers, motor analyzers, chassis charts, and pressure gauges.

- Inspect, repair, and maintain automotive and mechanical equipment and machinery, such as: pumps and compressors.

Wages & Employment Trends

National:

Median wages (2011): $20.02 hourly, $41,640 annual
Employment (2010): 242,000 employees
Projected growth (2010-2020): Average (10– 19%)
Projected Job Openings (2010-2020): 87,800

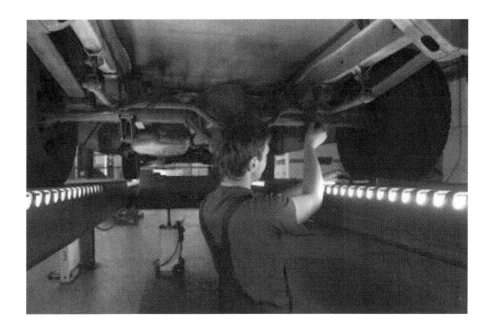

First-Line Supervisor of Mechanics, Installers, and Repairers
Directly supervise and coordinate the activities of mechanics, installers, and repairers.

Tasks:

- Determine schedules, sequences, and assignments for work activities, based on work priority, quantity of equipment, and skill of personnel.

- Monitor employees' work levels and review work performance.

- Monitor tool and part inventories and the condition and maintenance of shops to ensure adequate working conditions.

- Investigate accidents or injuries and prepare reports of findings.

- Recommend or initiate personnel actions, such as: hires, promotions, transfers, discharges, or disciplinary measures.

- Compile operational or personnel records, such as: time and production records, inventory data, repair or maintenance statistics, or test results.

- Develop, implement, or evaluate maintenance policies and procedures.

- Counsel employees about work-related issues and assist employees to correct job-skill deficiencies.

- Examine objects, systems, or facilities and analyze information to determine needed installations, services, or repairs.

- Conduct or arrange for worker training in safety, repair, or maintenance techniques, operational procedures, or equipment use.

Wages & Employment Trends

National:

    Median wages (2011): $28.77 hourly, $59,850 annual

    Employment (2010): 431,000 employees

    Projected growth (2010-2020): Average (10– 19%)

    Projected Job Openings (2010-2020): 164,900

Mobile Heavy Equipment Mechanics, Except Engines
Diagnose, adjust, repair, or overhaul mobile mechanical, hydraulic, and pneumatic equipment, such as: cranes, bulldozers, graders, and conveyors, used in construction, logging, and surface mining.

Tasks:

- Repair and replace damaged or worn parts.

- Dismantle and reassemble heavy equipment, using hoists and hand tools.

- Operate and inspect machines or heavy equipment to diagnose defects.

- Test mechanical products and equipment after repair or assembly to ensure proper performance and compliance with manufacturers' specifications.

- Clean, lubricate, and perform other routine maintenance work on equipment and vehicles.

- Read and understand operating manuals, blueprints, and technical drawings.

- Overhaul and test machines or equipment to ensure operating efficiency.

- Fit bearings to adjust, repair, or overhaul mobile mechanical, hydraulic, and pneumatic equipment.

- Diagnose faults or malfunctions to determine required repairs, using engine diagnostic equipment, such as: computerized test equipment and calibration devices.

- Examine parts for damage or excessive wear, using micrometers and gauges.

Wages & Employment Trends

National:

> **Median wages (2011):** $21.92 hourly, $45,600 annual
>
> **Employment (2010):** 125,000 employees
>
> **Projected growth (2010-2020):** Average (10– 19%)
>
> **Projected Job Openings (2010-2020):** 52,500

Heavy and Tractor-Trailer Truck Drivers

Drive a tractor-trailer combination or a truck with a capacity of at least twenty-six thousand pounds Gross Vehicle Weight (GVW). May be required to unload truck. Requires commercial driver's license.

Tasks:

- Inspect product load for accuracy and safely move it around the warehouse or facility to ensure timely and complete delivery.

- Move controls to drive gasoline- or electric-powered trucks, cars, or tractors and transport materials between loading, processing, and storage areas.

- Move levers or controls that operate lifting devices, such as: forklifts, lift beams with swivel-hooks, hoists, or elevating platforms, to load, unload, transport, or stack material.

- Position lifting devices under, over, or around loaded pallets, skids, or boxes and secure material or products for transport to designated areas.

- Manually or mechanically load or unload materials from pallets, skids, platforms, cars, lifting devices, or other transport vehicles.

- Perform routine maintenance on vehicles or auxiliary equipment, such as: cleaning, lubricating, recharging batteries, fueling, or replacing liquefied-gas tank.

- Weigh materials or products and record weight or other production data on tags or labels.

- Operate or tend automatic stacking, loading, packaging, or cutting machines.

- Turn valves and open chutes to dump, spray, or release materials from dump cars or storage bins into hoppers.

- Signal workers to discharge, dump, or level materials.

Wages & Employment Trends

National:

    Median wages (2011): $14.43 hourly, $30,010 annual

    Employment (2010): 522,000 employees

    Projected growth (2010-2020): Average (10–19%)

    Projected Job Openings (2010-2020): 209,500

Light Truck or Delivery Services Driver

Drive a light vehicle, such as a truck or van, with a capacity of less than twenty-six thousand pounds Gross Vehicle Weight (GVW), primarily to deliver or pick up merchandise or to deliver packages. May load and unload vehicle.

Tasks:

- Obey traffic laws and follow established traffic and transportation procedures.

- Inspect and maintain vehicle supplies and equipment, such as: gas, oil, water, tires, lights, or brakes, to ensure that vehicles are in proper working condition.

- Report any mechanical problems encountered with vehicles.

- Present bills and receipts and collect payments for goods delivered or loaded.

- Load and unload trucks, vans, or automobiles.

- Verify the contents of inventory loads against shipping papers.

- Turn in receipts and money received from deliveries.

- Maintain records, such as vehicle logs, records of cargo, or billing statements, in accordance with regulations.

- Read maps and follow written or verbal geographic directions

- Report delays, accidents, or other traffic and transportation situations to bases or other vehicles, using telephones or mobile two-way radios.

Wages & Employment Trends

National:

    Median wages (2011): $17.39 hourly, $36,180 annual

    Employment (2010): 732,000 employees

    Projected growth (2010-2020): Average (10–19%)

    Projected Job Openings (2010-2020): 311,700

Industrial Truck and Tractor Operator
Operate industrial trucks or tractors equipped to move materials around a warehouse, storage yard, factory, construction site, or similar location.

Tasks:

- Inspect product load for accuracy and safely move it around the warehouse or facility to ensure timely and complete delivery.

- Move controls to drive gasoline or electric-powered trucks, cars, or tractors and transport materials between loading, processing, and storage areas.

- Move levers or controls that operate lifting devices, such as: forklifts, lift beams with swivel-hooks, hoists or elevating platforms, to load, unload, transport or stack material.

- Position lifting devices under, over, or around loaded pallets, skids, or boxes and secure material or products for transport to designated areas.

- Manually or mechanically load or unload materials from pallets, skids, platforms, cars, lifting devices, or other transport vehicles.

- Perform routine maintenance on vehicles or auxiliary equipment, such as: cleaning, lubricating, charging batteries, fueling, or replacing liquefied gas tank.

- Weigh materials or products and record weight or other production data on tags or labels.

- Operate or tend automatic stacking, loading, packaging, or cutting machines.

- Turn valves and open chutes to dump, spray, or release materials from dump cars or storage bins into hoppers.
- Signal workers to discharge, dump, or level materials.

Wages & Employment Trends

National:

    Median wages (2011): $14.43 hourly, $30,010 annual

    Employment (2010): 522,000 employees

    Projected growth (2010-2020): Average (10–19%)

    Projected Job Openings (2010-2020): 209,500

15: Important Concepts Relating to Energy, Power and Automotive Industries

The purpose of this section is to offer a person a fundamental understanding of the concepts, terms and definitions and their applications in the real world. Once the person "gets into it," further educational programs are offered in technical schools, colleges, and universities. The author has vast knowledge of the math, physics, and other related sciences involved in these concepts; certainly, it will be minimized for quicker understanding before diving into it technically. After all, at this stage the critical issue is to look forward into new and emerging careers rather than looking at mathematical equations; no doubt, this will happen when the person decides to advance toward engineering degrees and up-to-date technology.

The concepts bring forward language arts and vocabulary enrichment when the person enters into the job market and starts conversing with employers of related industries. The following terms and concepts apply for the Energy-Power and Automotive technologies.

1. Energy:
The universe is made of energy and mass. Neither of them can be created or destroyed. It is possible to convert energy into different forms, such

as into heat (combustion of fuel in engines) or into radiant energy, such as microwave ovens.

On planet Earth, energy is found everywhere. It is available to all of us in the form of wind, solar, hydro, geothermal, and fossil fuels such as: coal, gasoline, and natural gases. Also, renewable sources played an important part of "early man" when he burned wood for survival. Engineers and scientists had to come up with many ideas on how to measure energy. The following will give the reader an idea how extensive it could be.

Conversion Factors for:
Energy—Work—Heat
1 m-kgf=9.807 joules   1 watt-sec=1 joule= 1 nt-m

	Btu	Ft-lb	Hp-hr	Joules	cal	Kw-hr
1 British thermal unit	1	777.9	3.929×10^{-4}	1055	252.0	2.930×10^{-4}
1 foot-pound	1.285×10^{-3}	1	5.051×10^{-7}	1.356	0.3239	3.766×10^{-7}
1 horsepower-hour	2545	1.980×10^{6}	1	2.685×10^{6}	6.414×10^{5}	0.7457
1 joule	9.484×10^{-4}	0.7376	3.725×10^{-7}	1	0.2389	2.778×10^{-7}
1 calorie	3.968×10^{-3}	3.087	1.559×10^{-6}	4.186	1	1.163×10^{-6}
1 kilowatt-hour	3413	2.655×10^{6}	1.341	3.6×10^{6}	8.601×10^{5}	1

2. Power/Horsepower:

The definition of power can easily be understood when you visualize a person pushing a car or lifting a weight. The question comes up: but how fast? This brings up the issue of force, distance, and time. When a person carries a sandbag to shore up flooding, that person did the work and carried the sandbag from point A to B. This is called the work done. Either slower or faster, it does not make any difference. For example, the sandbag weighed fifty-five pounds, and the distance the person moved it was ten feet; then, the work done is: **55lbs X 10ft=550ft-lb** of work. How fast was the work done? If 550 foot-pounds of work was done in ten seconds, then the power is equal to **550ft-lb/10 sec.**, or if the bag was moved in only one second, then the power is **550ft-lb/1 sec.**

Therefore:

$$\textbf{Power = work/time}$$

OR

$$\textbf{1 HP = 550 ft-lb/sec}$$

Conversion Factors for Power:

	Btu	Ft-lb/sec	hp	WATTS
I British thermal unit per hour	1	0.2161	3.929×10^{-4}	0.2930
1 foot-pound per minute	7.713×10^{-2}	1.667×10^{2}	3.030×10^{-5}	2.260×10^{-2}
1 foot-pound per second	4.628	1	1.818×10^{-3}	1.356
1 horsepower	2545	550	1	745.7
1 calorie per second	14.29	3.087	5.613×10^{-3}	4.186
1 kilowatt	3413	737.6	1.341	1000
1 watt	3.413	0.7376	1.341×10^{-3}	1

3. Mass:

It is very common to use weight in pounds (lbs.) or kilograms (kg) when groceries are bought in a store. However, what is *not* known is that this one pound of purchase (i.e., steak) will weigh much less on the moon. US astronauts that landed on the moon would have felt cheated to see that their pound of steak weighed so much less. This brings up the term mass which indicates that the pound of steak still has the same mass but not weight. Newton discovered that the earth's gravitational pull has something to do with it.

When a race car accelerates, it is shown that the energy (fuel type used) is converted to power (engine horsepower) which accelerates the car (mass). This relationship is indicated by:

$$F=MA$$

Remember, the same race car will have different acceleration depending on which planet it is on, as shown here:

Body	Mass (Earth = 1)	Distance from Sun (Miles)	Diameter (Miles)	Acceleration Due to Gravity at Surface (Ft/sec²)
Sun	329,390	-	864,100	900.3
Mercury	0.0549	36.0×10^6	3,194	12.9
Venus	0.8073	67.1×10^6	7,842	28.9
Earth	1.0000	92.9×10^6	7,926	32.2
Mars	0.1065	141.7×10^6	4,263	12.9
Jupiter	314.5	483.4×10^6	89,229	86.8
Saturn	94.07	886.1×10^6	74,937	38.6
Uranus	14.40	1782.7×10^6	33,181	32.2
Neptune	16.72	2793.1×10^6	30,882	32.2
Moon	0.01228	[b]23.9×10^4	2,159.9	5.47

4. Physical Properties

The following information is helpful for the understanding of air and its composition. Automotive performance is affected by air density, temperature, pressure, and altitude. Auto industry engineers need to know these properties to be able to design electronics and compensate for the various conditions in the air.

Composition of Dry Air at Earth's Surface:

Element	Density at 0°C, 760 torrs, g/liter	Percent by volume	Molecular weight (0 = 16.000)
Nitrogen (N^2)	1.2506	78.08	28.016
Oxygen (O^2)	1.4290	20.95	32.000
Argon (Ar)	1.7837	.93	39.944
Carbon Dioxide (Co^2)	1.9769	.03	44.010
Neon (Ne)	0.9004	1.8×10^{-3}	20.183
Helium (He)	0.1785	5.2×10^{-4}	4.003
Krypton (Kr)	3.708	1.0×10^{-4}	83.7
Hydrogen (H^2)	0.0899	5.0×10^{-5}	2.016
Xenon (Xe)	5.851	8.0×10^{-6}	131.3
Ozone (O^3)	2.22	1.0×10^{-6}	48.000

Physical Properties:

Density of Air (STP)	=	1.29 kg/meter^3
Density of Water (20°C)	=	1.00 x 103 kg/meter3
Density of Mercury (20°C)	=	13.5 x 103 kg/meter3
Heat of Fusion of Water (0°C)	=	79.7 cal/gm
Heat of Vaporization of Water (100°C)	=	540 cal/gm
Standard Atmosphere	=	1.01 x 105 nt/meter2 = 14.7 lb/in2
Speed of Sound in Dry Air (STP)	=	331 meters/sec = 1090 ft/sec

| | Acceleration of Gravity (Standard) | = | $9.81 \text{ meters/sec}^2 = 32.2 \text{ ft/sec}^2$ |

Acceleration of Gravity (Standard) = $9.81 \text{ meters/sec}^2 = 32.2 \text{ ft/sec}^2$

Mean Radius of Earth = $6.37 \times 10^6 \text{ meters} = 3960 \text{ miles}$

Mean Earth-Sun Distance = $1.49 \times 10^8 \text{ km} = 92.9 \times 10^6 \text{ miles}$

Mean Earth–Moon Distance = $3.80 \times 10^5 \text{ km} = 2.39 \times 10^5 \text{ miles}$

5. Pressure

In a car engine, the cylinder pressure acting on the piston creates the force needed to turn the crankshaft. Therefore, the pressure is the bottom line of what the cylinder sees. In a diesel engine, the high pressure required to ignite the fuel is the key factor for the combustion process.

A turbocharger increases the mass of air entering the engine, which increases the combustion pressure. The term pressure is a vital measurement for all living creatures and machines. The air pressure diminishes rapidly as aircraft climb high altitudes, which are compensated for by compressing air into the cabin area.

In a hydro-plant, the pressure at the bottom of a dam is what engineers measure. They call it the "head" pressure of the dam. This is an important factor so that auto industry can let you know what your tire pressure should be for safe and economic reasons.

	Atm	Inch of water	Lb/in.^{2}
1 atmosphere =	1	406.8	14.70
1 inch of water at 4°C^a =	2.458×10^{-3}	1	3.613×10^{-2}
1 pound per in.^{2}	6.805×10^{-2}	27.68	1

[a] Where the acceleration of gravity has the standard value 9.80665 meters/sec^2

6. Combustion

The combustion of fuels is a very complex subject. Important considerations are listed (partially) to bring awareness to the reader that scientists and engineers are constantly working to improve the "total" burning of a fuel. For example, fuel can burn "openly" in a power-generating plant. These fuels can be coal, diesel, and natural gas, that burn without compressing the air. We categorize these as external combustion, compared to internal combustion engines: where the piston compresses the air before ignition.

The concept of compressing the air and then igniting the fuel brings a vast change in fuel emissions and efficiencies. This is why diesel engines can operate at higher efficiencies. Gas engines have increased the compression ratios so that they too get better combustion and higher efficiencies. Combustion of fuels is effected by:

1. Compression ratio of engines

2. Type of ignition used (spark as compression ignition)

3. Ignition timing

4. Atmospheric conditions

5. Energy content (Btu's/lb)

6. Discharge pressure of burned/unburned fuel

7. Many other factors beyond the scope of this book

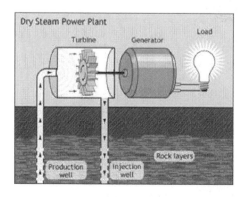
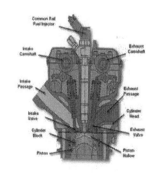

7. Energy Storage

In this book, several types of energy storage systems were discussed/ presented. This subject could require Mechanical/Electrical/Chemical Engineering graduates to fully appreciate the extent of the subject and how best to match the storage capacity to the demand on the user end. The intent here is to bring to the forefront the important types of energy storage systems and have the reader develop a basic vocabulary and knowledge.

The mechanical types of storage have been in use with clocks and springs for over a century. It is the stress in a torsion bar that stores the energy. The chemical storage is common with car batteries and electric cars. They have been used for over a century. The energy stored in lakes behind a dam is vast and highly beneficial for hydro-plants. Some sites use their extra power to pump water into other reservoirs for future use. Solar thermal installations have increased the demand for hot water tanks, which store the sun's energy for domestic hot water needs.

Water represents the cheapest way of storing energy, because the total energy in Btu's is simply calculated by:

Total Btu's in the tank =   lbs of water in the tank x Temp. rise in °F

This means that for each one pound of water the temperature rises in degrees Fahrenheit, one Btu is stored.

If the water tank holds three hundred pounds, and the solar panels raise the temperature from seventy degrees Fahrenheit to 170 degrees Fahrenheit, the temperature rise is one hundred degrees Fahrenheit. This means:

$$\text{Total Btu's stored} = 300 \text{ lbs x } 100 \text{ °F Rise}$$
$$= 30,000 \text{ Btu's}$$

Similarly, the dam holds its potential energy determined solely by its height, because water density is the constant.

$P = \rho h$

P = potential energy

ρ = density of water

h = height of the lake to the turbine discharge

8. Torque

The auto industry is the largest user of the terms "torque" and "horsepower." Consumers are impressed when both figures are high compared with other cars. The reason is obvious: both readings are crucial for a high performance car in terms of acceleration.

Another common item included with a car is a spare tire and a torque wrench. Have you noticed that a longer handle makes the nuts on the tires come off easier than a short-handled one?

Torque is defined as:

$T = F \times d$

Where: T = Torque in FT-LB

F = Force perpendicular to moment arm in LBF

d = Moment arm in feet

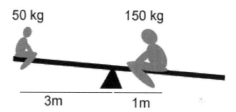

50 kg   150 kg

3m   1m

An equilibrium exists when:

Weight x d1 = d2 x F

This simple relationship will show the reader the advantage when d2 gets to be longer.

9. **Energy in Motion**

When two cars collide, the damage on each car can be described as "absorbing" the other car's momentum/its kinetic energy. There are several terms that need to be explained.

Momentum

When a large car has a lot of weight (MASS)—say, M1 going at a speed of forty-five miles per hour (the speed given by symbol V1)—we describe its momentum as M1xV1.

Now, if a smaller car with a mass (M2) is going slower as V2, the momentum will be M2xV2. When they collide, the M1V1=M2V2; however, the bigger car has more momentum and extra energy, known as energy in motion. This extra energy will show up on the smaller car as a bigger damage (due to absorption); plus, it will be kicked off further. Because energy cannot be created or destroyed, it translates into crushing the car's frame and body. For cars that travel on highways at a constant speed, we can estimate their energy by $1/2mv^2$. This is known as kinetic energy. The important point made here is that when a car doubles the speed, the kinetic energy increases by a factor of four.

Collisions are defined as "elastic" collision or "inelastic" collision. An inelastic collision is observed when on a pool table: two balls collide and recover their speed (relatively) compared with a ball that is made of "putty." Certainly, the putty absorbs the energy to itself: just as a car can absorb a collision into its frame/body. The kinetic energy (E) is mathematically given as

$$E_{Kinetic} = \frac{1}{2} mv^2$$

Where: v is the velocity in ft/sec

m is the mass/weight of vehicle

Engineers design vehicles having all these factors in mind to minimize humans' absorbing the energy and letting the car get the brunt by using materials and bumpers that serve this purpose.

10. Aerodynamics

All race cars are designed to reduce the drag forces on the car. Also, consumers that buy cars notice the aerodynamics involved in the design. There are engineers who can test the vehicles in a wind tunnel and find out what part of the car should be re-designed. About one hundred years ago, cars/airplanes were hardly designed with good shapes to consider the effects of drag on cars/airplanes. Now, all cars are tested in wind tunnels to reduce drag and increase fuel mileage.

Aerodynamicists are those people that can apply important principles to many applications beyond just testing vehicles. For example, bridges and tall buildings are tested in wind tunnels to find problems that may cause instability through vibrations. Today's airplanes, both sonic and supersonic aircraft, are designed by engineers who specialize in aircraft industries. It should be clear to the reader that aerodynamic "loads" are calculated by these specialists, who are very aware of the impact of high-speed winds on cars and buildings.

11. Area and Volume

The world uses two different scales of measurement.

The metric system is used by mostly European, ~~Russian~~, and many other countries.

Imperial system is used by many "original" English-speaking countries.

To convert from one form to another requires some understanding of key conversion factors. For example, in weighing an item, people use the term pound (lb.); in the metric system, they use kilogram (kg). For distance, it is feet (ft) and meters (m) respectively, for the metric system. The conversion is as follows:

Length:　　　　　One (1) foot = 12 inches x 2.54 cm/in = 30.48 cm
　　　　　　　　　One Inch = 2.54 cm
Mass (weight):　　1 Kilogram = 2.205 lbs
Area = length x width
Volume = length x width x height
Circular Area = πr^2 where r is the radius OR $\pi D^2/4$ since D is diameter = 2r

You need to know math to calculate the volume of a cylinder at the top of the compression stroke and at the bottom of the stroke to derive the compression ratio of an engine. This term is very important in knowing how efficient an engine is—especially for diesel engines.

Compression Ratio = Volume (at bottom of stroke, divided by volume on top of stroke)

The following conversion factors can help the reader to use/convert metric units to the English system:

AREA	meter^2	cm^2	ft^2	in.^{2}
1 square meter =	1	10^4	10.76	1550
1 square centimeter =	10^{-4}	1	1.076×10^{-3}	0.1550
1 square foot =	9.290×10^{-2}	929.0	1	144
1 square inch =	6.452×10^{-4}	6.452	6.944×10^{-3}	1

1 square mile = 27,878,400 ft^2 = 640 acres   1 acre = 43,560 ft^2

VOLUME	meter^3	cm^3	1 (liter)	ft^3	in.^{3}
1 cubic meter =	1	10^6	1000	35.31	6.102×10^4
1 cubic centimeter =	10^{-6}	1	1.000×10^{-3}	3.531×10^{-5}	6.102×10^{-2}
1 liter =	1.000×10^{-3}	1000	1	3.531×10^{-2}	61.02
1 cubic foot =	2.832×10^{-2}	2.832×10^4	28.32	1	1728
1 cubic inch =	1.639×10^{-5}	16.39	1.639×10^{-2}	5.787×10^{-4}	1

1 US fluid gallon = 4 US fluid quarts = 8 US pints = 128 US fluid ounces = 231 in.^{3}

1 British imperial gallon = the volume of 10 lb of water at 62°F = 277.42 in.^{3}

1 liter = the volume of 1 kg of water at its maximum density = 1000.028 cm^3

1 liter = 1000 cm^3

Mass:

1 kg "=" 2.205 lb on Earth

12. Hydraulics

Automobile brakes use hydraulic fluids. This brings up an important definition/observation that these fluids/liquids are not compressible, like air/gas. This is why people study the "behavior" of fluids (hydraulics) versus gas (pneumatics). As a matter of fact, no gas should be in the hydraulic lines of vehicles. This will cause "spongy," soft brake pedal behavior. Other differences are very noticeable: the liquids can hold more heat than air/cubic foot. The viscosity is another major difference that characterizes hydraulics versus pneumatics. Power transmission with hydraulics is immediate compared to gases—especially hydraulic motors/pistons.

In terms of application, when force is applied on a brake pedal, there is an interesting point to make: even though there are four wheels/brakes, the pressure is the same as shown here.

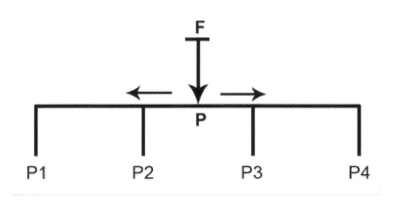

$$F = P \times A$$

Where: Pressure (P) x Area (A) = F
However, $P = P1 = P2 = P3 = P4$

Now, the driver is assured that all brakes have identical pressure. The same pressure would have happened if air were used, but it would have required a much longer pedal—not realistic!

13. Electricity and Conductors

When an energy source (i.e., car battery) needs to provide power to crank an engine, we talk about current and voltage. However, we need to understand resistance to the flow of current. This resistance depends on: what types of conductors are used, the diameter of the wire, the temperature, and the contacts between the two points. The relationship between voltage, current, and resistance was established by a well-known scientist/physicist: a German-born man, named Ohm. What he discovered is that electrical currents (I), now called amps (A) for short, flow through cables just like water will flow through pipes. The second aspect was that the flow rate was increased by pressure, called voltage (V). I am sure you are very familiar with fire trucks increasing the water pressure with a pump and having the water rate increase accordingly. Ohm's Law came into effect by a simple formula.

Ohm's Triangle

Cover the variable you want to find and perform
the resulting calculation *(Multiplication/Division)*
as indicated.

Car batteries are mostly twelve volts, and loss of power is purely the result of the resistance in a circuit. The resistance in a circuit can be symbolized by a water valve in a hose. If the valve is partially closed, the water pressure is diminished, including the water flow. Try to note this relationship in a shower.

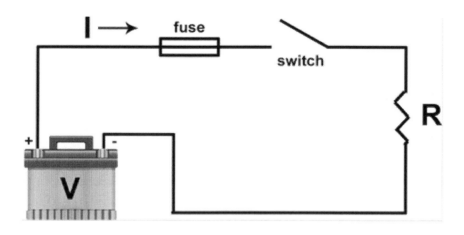

Measurements: It is possible to measure voltage, amperage, and resistance with a multimeter. The amps can be done by having the current flow through the meter set for amps, just as water meters measure the flow in pipes. The voltage is pressure: from the high point to the ground. This was shown in the case of Hoover Dam, where water pressure reaches zero at the discharge level to the river. If two measurements are known, the third is calculated from I = E/R. So, you need to learn a little more of math if you happen to have series circuits, parallel circuits, or a combination of both.

Let's look at a series circuit. If there are more lights installed on the circuit—such as headlights and brake lights—then the first one will have the brightest light, and the last one will have the dimmest. This is not acceptable. It is calculated by adding all the resistive elements (or loads, as they are called in technical language), and OHM's Law is used to figure out the current. The battery voltage is constant at twelve volts. If each resistance is equal to 1.5 Ohms for headlights (two lamps), then the total resistance is three Ohms. Then, the formula reads:

$$I = \frac{E}{R} = \frac{12V}{3 \text{ ohms}} = 4 \text{amps}$$

In a series circuit, both lamps will cause a pressure drop/voltage drop noted as IR drop. If the current is four amps and R=1.5, the voltage drops to six volts for the first and the second lamp, as well for the total battery voltage drop of twelve volts down to zero volts.

What about the parallel circuit? Concept #12 discussed how pressure is applied to all wheels so that the brakes see the same pressure.

This same circuit can apply to electrical measurements.

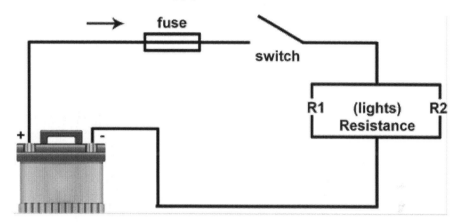

Ohm's Law can be shown to apply if we do the math and find out the total resistance (R_T) for this circuit. The formula is:

$$R_T = \frac{R1 \quad x \quad R2}{R_1 \quad + \quad R_2}$$

If the circuit has more than two resistances, the formula becomes:

$$R_T = \frac{1}{R_1} + \frac{1}{R_2} + \frac{1}{R_3} \text{ and so on.}$$

The rest of it is simple math and the substitution of values. When R_T is summed up, then the formula I=E/R takes effect.

14. Ignition Timing

When the spark plug fires inside the cylinder at a certain point during the piston travel to ignite the fuels, this spark initiates the combustion process as shown here with the Megatech oil-less, transparent engine. It is possible to preset the timing or make it variable. But this process is defined by the rotation of the crankshaft in a full circle of 360 degrees. During the compression stroke, the piston travels upward: right before it reaches the top, the spark plug can be set to fire. This is known as X degrees advance ignition. While the fuel starts igniting, the piston continues to compress the gas, until it reaches the top and reverses the direction.

**Megatech Transparent engine showing
the 4-Stroke Combustion Cycle**

It is possible to set the spark plug to fire at top dead center: at zero degrees. Now, we have defined another condition to compare what happens to the engine performance, emission, and fuel economy.

The third physical process is when the spark plug fires after top dead center. This position is known as "retarding" the ignition after top dead center.

The crankshaft rotation is known as going through one full circle, which is 360 degrees.

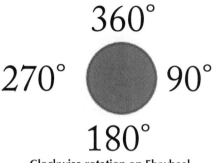

Clockwise rotation on Flywheel

What effect does the ignition timing have on the engine?

The following factors can be studied, observed, and measured with the Megatech oil-less, transparent engine. Ignition timing causes the following effects.

1. Engine torque and RPM: Both of these factors are the result of full combustion after the compression stroke. The fuel starts igniting ahead of time before the piston reaches the top dead center and continues through the power and then the exhaust stroke. This effect can be measured by the dynamometer.

2. Fuel efficiency: The best results are achieved before the piston reaches top dead center. It takes time for the fuel to burn, instead of "explode" (i.e., in pre-ignition/gas-knock). This burning of fuel is what we need for better mileage.

3. Emissions: EPA regulations for emission standards are set, and all cars are tested for their emissions. When an emissions analyzer is inserted into the tailpipe of a car, it is measuring

the combustion products and unburned fuel. The ignition timing has considerable effect on emissions, as it does for the horsepower output (engine torque X RPM). Which one do you compromise? We call this "trade-off:" between engine power versus emissions.

4. Combustion temperature: When the fuel mixture is ignited, it causes the flame front to move into the piston. Since "advancing" the timing causes a longer time for the piston to travel, the fuel is burning longer and, at the same time, is initially being heated while still being compressed. This combustion causes both the pressure and the temperature to go up! When automotive engineers design a car, they study the thermodynamics and then build a prototype to test the theory.

There are different fuels with differing effects on the engine. For example, what happens if alcohol is injected with the gasoline fuel? What if engines are run with hydrogen and oxygen? This is why technical people are constantly searching for answers to alternative fuels. What about electric cars? This is a new front in the automotive industry: which will depend on electric generating plants and their policies.

15. Atomization of Fuel

It should be stated that when fuel burns inside the cylinder, rather than explodes, it is called "gas knock." There are good reasons why automotive engineers are looking for the better of two worlds: better fuel economy and lower emissions.

When we look at the process of fuel burning, we are actually examining from a molecular point of view: which is the phenomenon of interaction between the air (oxygen supply) and fuel. In order for the fuel to burn, it needs oxygen (oxidizer) to come into fuel contact. This brings up an issue of surface area. If you look into the water drop of a faucet, you can see its size. If you vaporize it into steam, water has not changed—except its droplets and temperature. This means that the surface area is exposed a lot more in a droplet than in a drop of water. So, the physical process of breaking up the drop into thousands of droplets is known as atomization.

There are many ways of doing this. It requires technical knowledge as to how it is done. However, these are the methods used to achieve atomization:

1. Mechanical: High-pressure fuel injection into a diesel engine has been known to work. The same principal applies to the gas engine, with direct fuel injection. In this diagram, a fuel pump is used to Increase the pressure and atomize the fuel.

2. Ultrasonic: This concept has been tested and shown that it works with common products, such as humidifiers. Sound waves travel just like water waves and can be heard. An aircraft that travels faster than the speed of sound creates shock waves. These can crack windows or even walls of homes. The same effect can cause drops of fuels to be

broken up to tiny droplets (atomized) and have them readily be mixed with oxygen.

3. Electromagnetic waves: Most of the public is familiar with microwave ovens. Certainly, the energy is used up by the food being heated and cooked. The energy level and wavelength can be controlled electronically to atomize the fuel once it is injected into the cylinder. As a matter of fact, you might not even need a spark plug if you were to use microwaves to ignite the fuel. This wave can be timed just like a spark plug before, at, or after "to dead center."

16. Electric Vehicles versus Nuclear Utilities

In order to obtain clean emissions, the auto industry is promoting the use of electric vehicles. The intent is very good: they can design and produce these cars very efficiently. What are the other elements to consider?

1.) Changing of batteries

2.) What is the source of the energy the power plant depends on: coal or solar?

3.) Life cycle of the batteries

4.) Charging station locations and infrastructure

5.) Cost of electricity

6.) Other factors, such as: range, safety, service issues, etc.

Initially, a lot was presented in regard to the operating principles of power stations; for example: how a hydro-plant works, how wind farms operate (non-carbon-based fuels), and fossil fuels that are used as an energy source. The United States applied nuclear physics to civilian use for electric power generation, ships and submarines and for medical purposes. The nuclear power stations are in operation and are considered one of the most important options to replace coal burning or other fossil fuel plants. Since electric cars draw considerable power, it is best suited for nighttime charging: when power stations' outputs are reduced due to lack of demand.

The purpose of electric cars is to reduce carbon emissions. But, let's compare the nuclear energy versus coal for producing heat running the turbines. Once thermal (heat) energy is given off the nuclear reactor, the rest of the system is similar to coal-fired plants. The big difference is the energy source which gives off the heat.

1kg of uranium (u-235) = 3 million kg coal

A coal-fired one-thousand-megawatt power plant uses eight thousand tons of coal a day. This equals eight thousand tons (one thousand kilograms per ton), which equals eight million kilograms of coal. = 8000 tons (1000kg/ton) = 8,000,000 kg of coal. Now it becomes clear why some interest is emerging with nuclear plants.

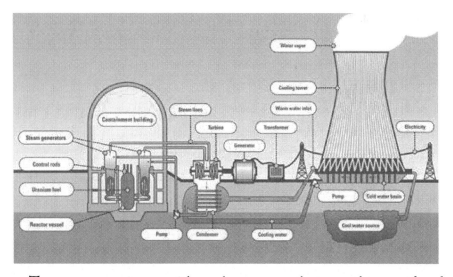

There are more issues with nuclear energy that must be considered, as follows:

1.) What should be done with the disposal of used nuclear fuel rods?

2.) What safety measures must be taken in case of emergency?

3.) What is the barrel cost of nuclear waste for a period of ten thousand years, or so?

Elements that nuclear reactors require are as follows:

1.) Nuclear reactor fuel and core design

2.) Control rods

3.) The coolant

4.) The vessel to contain the above elements

5.) Circulating pump

6.) Steam generator

7.) Steam turbine

8.) Condenser for the steam

9.) Control panels, safety system, and more.

It is not an easy task compared to solar PV panels that can be dismantled and safely recycled/ disposed. Now it is clear why there is no one particular source for "power-hungry" electric cars to meet the demand for electricity.

17. Friction

In a vehicle, there are many areas that cause loss of power, and the driver pays at the end with more fuel consumed and a loss of mileage. The intent here is to identify major parts that cause frictional losses. There are several categories of friction.

1. Surface friction: This is dependent on what kinds of materials are used and for what purpose. The coefficient factor μ (Mu) is a Greek symbol used to denote the particular property of that surface. The formula is expressed as:

    $F = \mu N$

    F – Applied force
    N – Is normal/perpendicular force to the surface

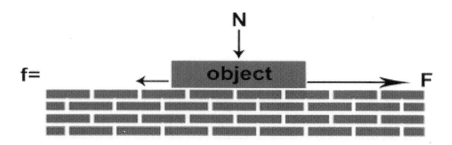

As this formula shows, the applied force (F) should overcome the N (weight) x μ (factor) before movement starts. This is known as the "static" frictional force. Any higher force (F) applied to the object starts the acceleration in accordance with Newton's Law: F=ma. The μ factor depends on the material used at room temperature. For example, the brake pads have a larger μ factor than a glazed surface material, such as: glass or ceramic.

2. Rolling friction: This has much less friction than sliding friction. Early humans had to push and pull solid rocks to move them into a particular location. Then they used trunks of trees

to roll them, and finally, the wheel came about. This is the same concept: cars use wheels to roll on the roads. There are many areas in a car that the reader should be aware of, such as: frictional losses and how engineers solve these problems.

a. Engine power loss: One of the biggest losses occurs when the cylinder wall and the piston come in contact. Considering the piston moves at high speeds up and down, considerable power is lost in the sliding friction. It makes sense to look into:

1. Ring materials that can stand high temperatures yet have low μ factors.

2. Cylinder walls made of materials and manufacturing process that give the surface a smooth finish and a low μ factor.

3. Pistons that are made of materials that can take the dynamic loads of the combustion chamber pressure and temperature yet have a low μ factor.

When the above factors are all considered, the next step is to look for a lubricant that lowers the frictional losses. Engineers address these issues and provide choices that are acceptable in the cost to manufacture.

b. Crankcase: In an engine—single or multi-cylinder engine—the crankcase has a reservoir of oil to lubricate the bearings and reduce the temperature of the surfaces in the ball bearings. There are certain types of engines that use roller bearings, needle bearings, or ball bearings. They all serve a special purpose. In all cases, they represent losses of power.

c. Transmissions: Another major point is the transmission where the power has to be sent to the wheels in the rear, front, or all four wheels. Certainly this is another major area of power loss, and engineers are consistently designing better ways of minimizing the losses, yet matching the power to acceleration needs of the car (load matching). It is a major challenge to design the proper transmission for the type of engine torque and speed—should it be three speeds or an eight-speed transmission?

d. Aerodynamics: Yes, air has friction and contributes to the power loss of the engine. This subject is very complex and is a specialty of the aerodynamicist, who can model the car and put it in a wind tunnel for testing the "drag forces."

e. Wheels/Tires: Another area that tire manufacturers constantly research for is finding materials that have lower friction, yet they can configure it so it does not hydroplane.

f. Driving habits: Stop and go in traffic is a wasted energy in frictional losses in the brakes. Here, you need materials with long life, yet higher frictional surfaces that absorb the braking energy. This factor adds to loss of mileage, because friction produces wasted heat. However, hybrid cars use electrical dynamic braking which converts the so called "losses" into beneficial electrical energy, putting it back into the batteries.

18. Rocket Propulsion

The concept of rockets goes back many centuries with the Chinese fireworks: even today these fireworks use the same principles. Since this book is all about energy, power, and automotive technology, it is just as important that rockets are considered as transportation means from point A to B or into outer space. So, an energy conversion into useful power has been presented, including "air-breathing" internal combustion engines. The biggest difference between a rocket engine and a jet engine is the fact that a rocket engine has to carry its own "air" (or oxidizer) to burn the fuel on board. The intent here is to explain how this happens and build on the knowledge of internal combustion engines.

1. Comparing the combustion chamber of a rocket engine to a gas engine

A rocket engine has a combustion chamber, just as a piston engine has its own combustion chamber. When fuel burns inside a combustion chamber, it creates *pressure*. This pressure acts on all surface areas available. We know force = pressure x area. We also know that when force is applied to an object, it accelerates and moves on in the direction of the force.

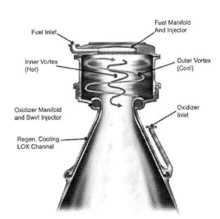

Gas Engine: Rocket Engine:

2. Gas Engine:

> F = Pressure x area
>
> F – Average pressure x area of piston
>
> The force is transmitted by the connecting rod to the crankshaft, which operates the wheels.

3. Rocket engine:

The combustion of the fuel inside the rocket engine creates pressure in the combustion chamber—no different from the gas engine. The <u>net pressure</u> in a rocket engine changes as it climbs out of the atmosphere. For the moment, let's assume the rocket is on the ground and ready for launch. The "net" pressure acting on the inside of the rocket engine, multiplied by the effective area, is a net force, called the thrust. Let's assume that the internal pressure of the rocket engine is 200 psi, and the gas engine is the same. The inside net surface area or the rocket engine is 100 square inches, then the force/thrust = 200 psi x 100 sq. in. = 20,000 lbs. of force. This thrust will force the rocket to lift if its weight is less than seventeen thousand pounds. (Note: usually thrust to weight ratio is 1.3/1.)

In the car engine, the same pressure will produce 200 psi x $\pi D^2/4$ where D is the piston diameter, in this case three inches.

$$200 \times \frac{3.12 \times (3)2}{4} = 4200 \text{ lbs of force}$$

In science, we apply Newton's Law: "for every action there is an equal and opposite reaction." If the rocket engine produces twenty thousand pounds of thrust, then it has to take off upward, just as the piston went down with a force of about forty-two hundred pounds. Outboard engines have a propeller that pushes the water in the opposite direction as the boat. This is an example of how Newton's Law applies to many situations.

A rocket engine during flight is best analyzed by other theories which consider the loss of weight of the rocket engine due to burning off fuel and oxidizer, thrust increase, less aerodynamic loads, etc. We all are familiar with a car accelerating by using Newton's Law (F=ma); likewise, the rocket is accelerating faster due to the decrease of mass (getting lighter).

Special Thanks
to
President Obama

who insisted on including Alternate Energy Sources as an additional
option for America's Energy Independence.

**During a visit to a college, President Obama looks at training
equipment designed by Vahan V. Basmajian and Megatech staff.**

Also:
Thanks to American Free Enterprise
which allows people to exercise their rights for entrepreneurship, freedom,
and self-development through education and training.